# YOUR SIGNS

## An Empowering Astrology Guide for 2020

Use the Movement of the Planets
to Navigate Life and Inform Decisions

Carolyne Faulkner

HARPER
DESIGN

An Imprint of HarperCollins Publishers

*To my teachers and to you, the reader*

*We have to care for ourselves, humanity and our beautiful home, Earth, in order to create new ways of living and more positive karma all round. Kindness is something that we really need to crank up and pump out into the world. This begins within and will instill a sense of belonging in us all, delivering much greater security in our crazy and equally fabulous and creative world.*

# Contents

For You, the Reader ........................................................................ iv

Dynamic Astrology™ ...................................................................... v

Our Time Is Now ........................................................................... vi

Your Journal, Your Birth Chart ................................................... x

January ............................................................................................ 1

February ........................................................................................ 30

March ............................................................................................. 58

April ................................................................................................ 84

May ............................................................................................... 110

June .............................................................................................. 137

July ............................................................................................... 164

August .......................................................................................... 193

September .................................................................................... 219

October ........................................................................................ 245

November ..................................................................................... 271

December ..................................................................................... 294

# For You, the Reader

ello, my name is Carolyne, and I am your translator, one who, more than anything, wishes you to learn and use astrology, the most beautiful language on Earth (French, Italian and Spanish are perhaps a close joint second). In this journal I offer you star knowledge, along with well-being tips that work and power tools that never lose their power, and I give you room for your own reflections, which will give your soul the chance to be heard and you the space to write down what it is saying.

I am so grateful for the karma that has brought me here. All the magic, turbulence and transitions in my own life have brought me to this very moment, and in this moment you and I are connecting. All the twists and turns on your own journey have led you here. Think for a moment about exactly how or why you discovered this journal and the series of events in your own life that directed you to it. That is karma, and it's magical – but more on that throughout, as I am very big on karma.

My journey so far has enabled me to be in the fortunate position to share not only the wisdom of the stars and my spiritual teachers with you, but also effective life coaching designed to enhance your everyday life and deepen your connectivity and receptivity overall. I am beyond thrilled to be alive and experiencing first-hand the spiritual revolution that has roused enough of a readership to warrant this journal! For so many years I, like many others, was advised to tone down my depth and wear a mask in order to survive. How times have delightfully changed.

We are only on this wonderful planet for a relatively short time, so make yours count. No matter who you are or what you do, be happy!

I am happy to enable everyone to skip over the complexities and start practicing the art of Dynamic Astrology™. Every word I write and tip I offer is laced with meaning and holds fast to the echoes of the ageless words and sage teachings of my great, mostly departed teachers. That's why this journal is dedicated to my teachers and to you, the reader.

It is a magical world, so live your very best life and enjoy every single day and, in a world where you can choose to be anything, choose to be you.

Enjoy!
Love from your friend,

*Carolyne Faulkner*

# Dynamic Astrology™

This is not just astrology, this is Dynamic Astrology™, a contemporary self-improvement method based on the ancient language of the stars. Dynamic Astrology™ is, without doubt, the result of an alchemical process. The motivation behind it, as well as the result, is pure gold.

You may ask why I am so passionate about the language of the stars. Quite frankly, it changed the game of life for me – and that's why I want to share it with as many people as possible. A deep love and innate understanding of astrology, combined with the passion to learn and the patience to reflect, changed the way I saw myself and transformed how I related to the people in my life and the everyday situations I faced; prior to this, I struggled.

With an understanding of your own birth chart (or someone else's), you can begin to cross-reference it with the astrology of the day and understand how the stars impact the way you feel, think and act. This can help you in many ways, for example, to stop taking things personally and ultimately allow more space for wisdom and compassion – and I absolutely love that. My late, great Buddhist master once told me, "There is nothing greater than compassion." This is such a simple lesson, there *is* nothing greater than compassion. Why? The energy of the universe acts as a magnet and brings us more of the same; so, if we are less judgmental of ourselves and others and kinder in all aspects of our life, then this is what we draw back. You can help make it happen. Astrology is wonderfully empowering, and when you harness it, it can feel as though you can press a "pause" button before responding to a situation and give yourself more space to check in with your higher mind. That space is crucial for empowering your moves and interactions to deliver better outcomes.

For me, astrology is the most powerful and magical language on Earth: it never discriminates, it helps us to attune to universal energy, which exists within us all, and, when used effectively, it has the capability to reconnect us to our most authentic self and illuminate our deeper path. I try not to make promises that cannot be kept, because doing that weakens the auric field of protection that we each have. But I can promise you that the journal you have in your hands will enhance your life, however you use it, inform you and help to prepare you for each month, week and day of this revolutionary year.

# Our Time Is Now

The highly prophesized shift in consciousness that took a hold in 2012 is awakening our thirst for spirituality without hypocrisy or hierarchy and our authentic connections to the universe and all other beings. Authenticity is an effective tonic for combating the emptiness of superficiality and discovering cool ways of translating ancient knowledge and decoding sacred systems such as astrology. I truly believe that in each of us there lies an immense source of untapped power, as well as unlimited potential for greatness. Within the cells of our body there are the remnants of stars that exploded. As blood courses through our veins, so does stardust.

We are all part of the universe, and the stars' movements and activities impact us all. Realizing this is a game changer. I would say that, wouldn't I? But this is the revolution, and it's one brimming with awareness, synchronicities and, above all, loving kindness, including toward ourselves. When the internal wars raging inside our mind reduce, then we positively shift the energy in our life and our environment. If we wish to live in peace and happiness, then our first step must be toward cultivating peace and happiness within. There is no better time than now.

Know that the future is not written. Nothing is fixed: everything changes, and so is impermanent, which also means that our past negative karma can be purified by our present deeds. Your future is pure potential based on your choices now. I don't believe that any star, god or man writes the future; it's solely ours to create. So, how do we do that? Through awareness and managing energy.

# Energy ... and Vibes

People often talk about "energy" and "vibes." Everything is energy, and astrology is a framework that we use to assess that energy, what it is and how it is manifesting. In many situations, with awareness of what is happening astrologically, we have the power to control, and even change, the energy and, significantly, our personal dynamics.

| *Energy:* | *Energies:* |
|---|---|
| *"our spirit and vibe and their* | *"feelings that evoke tension* |
| *impact on others"* | *or positive vibes"* |

Interestingly, there is scientific research out there that has concluded that the key to our own happiness lies in helping others. But before we can really help others, we first have to help ourselves. And we can begin by being kinder to our heart. The first step is to stop judging ourselves so harshly, to become more aware and to take the time to reflect on our situation, so that we have time to recognize choices and contemplate outcomes. We will also be able to recognize our potential and nurture our deeper, more authentic nature, and doing this will in turn give us a sense of purpose that will result in a skip to our step and a sense of knowing in our heart. It doesn't have to be grandiose or difficult – just one kind word can change someone's whole day, including our own. I have suggested some mantras and affirmations throughout this journal, but I do encourage you to regularly use your own.

# The Age of Aquarius (TAOA)

I believe that 2020 has rebooted the enlightened Age of Aquarius. Let me explain why! To really understand something, it's wise to study the history. There are many conflicting opinions around TAOA's actual start date, and some believe it began as far back as the early twentieth century. According to Helena Blavatsky, the nineteenth-century Russian occultist, philosopher, author and co-founder of the Theosophical Society, 1900 was "the commencement of the Aquarian Age" and a time when "the psychic idiosyncrasies of humanity will enter on a great change." Despite this, some people believe the Age of Aquarius is yet to begin, though it seems that no academic, astronomer or astrologer can quite agree on it. I have studied both the prevailing and past astrology, as well as current events, and listened to many masters speak on the topic, so perhaps this summary of my research and discoveries will provide the means for you to decide for yourself.

Aquarius is the sign that provides enlightenment and evokes revolution; it promotes equality, freedom, tolerance, humanitarian ideals, awareness and consciousness. It also triggers inventions, new technologies and most things that connect the masses, like the media and technology industries; and reaches out to connect with the multiverse and beyond. Think space travel. In short, it's anything that serves to awaken people to the "bigger picture." However, Aquarius also causes chaos and is extremely rebellious, which, let's face it, can either go wrong or spectacularly right!

So, before we go any deeper, let's pause and define what a "spiritual" person is. Ancient prophets said, in differing ways, "Treat others as you would have them treat you," and it's the same thing. Work, play, friendship, love, whatever, the same rule applies. And so we must also apply it to ourselves. Period.

Modern everyday life can be challenging for the sensitive folk among us, those who feel the pain of humanity and the suffering of the planet, but it's worth remembering that light cannot exist without darkness; it is the natural law of the universe, and where angels walk, demons follow. The rather highly prophesied "big shift in consciousness" that began in 2012 was also predicted to be the "end of time." We know of course that it was not the "end of time." But perhaps it was the "end of time" as we had known it. The year 2012 was bloody and violent, highlighting the need for humanity to adopt an attitude of tolerance and find new ways of handling negativity, and it possibly triggered a collective desire for a better, more unified world. A covert spiritual revolution swept through our weary world.

In 2012, for example, a fifteen-year-old angel stood up to oppressive Earthly demons, demanding the right for girls to be educated; America's first African-American president was re-elected; the UK hosted the Olympics, which pumped heart, soul and the results of great teamwork around the globe; the Arab Spring protests continued against fascistic regimes; and Silicon Valley began to promote daily meditation practice in the workplace as a "must," after a visit from a Buddhist monk. Many of us, all around the world, began to wake up and stop believing all that we heard from those in public positions of authority or what we saw in the media and to initiate the search for our own deeper truth.

Life-changing spiritual practices, such as meditation and yoga, are now commonplace once again and, when combined with the ability to use the universal language of the stars, provide a winning formula, one that promotes awareness: enhancing our connections to life, the rhythms of the universe and all that lies beyond.

Does this mean that 2012 was the dawning of the Age of Aquarius? Many say no, because it actually began in the 1960s. Perhaps it did. Saturn takes around twenty-eight years to complete a full cycle through the twelve astrological signs; Jupiter takes about twelve to thirteen years. By 1962 those planets were united in the sign of Aquarius.

And two years later, the Civil Rights Act was finally enacted in the US, ending racial segregation and promoting equal rights. Before the end of the decade, the first man walked on the Moon; the first transatlantic television signal was broadcast; an oral contraceptive was approved, giving women control over their own destinies, and the hippie movement took off, promoting peace, free love, music festivals and marijuana!

However, as far as I am concerned, 2020 is the real dawning of the Age of Aquarius. We have had a few trial runs, but this one is for real, as Saturn (the queen of the planets) and Jupiter (the great teacher) join the sign of Aquarius (the great awakener). Jupiter creates an expansive energy, Saturn provides structure and pragmatism, and Aquarius is all about the awakening of humanity, so this combination is rare and electrifying. You certainly won't be bored.

Nor will I. I feel that we are now back in the throes of TAOA, and it's exciting! These two magnificent and powerful planets are returning to the revolutionary sign of Aquarius for the first time since the 1960s, and this time we are more than prepared. We got this, 2020 journal!

# Your Journal, Your Birth Chart

Many Moons ago, astrology, my own soul and the incredible spiritual teachers that I trained with changed my life for the better. In turn I discovered, through experience, that helping others however I could (in my own way, and always creatively!) made *me* feel incredible, and I believe that sharing the know-how and giving back are the key to ultimate happiness. And so, new friend, I am honored to be your guide in the exciting months ahead.

# Your Journal

In this journal I have mapped out the astrology for the year 2020 and translated it into simple enough terms to be used in everyday life, guiding you through the shift in consciousness that is accelerating this year due to the Age of Aquarius. It works both on a spiritual and worldly basis, to steady and enhance your everyday life and nourish your soul. You can use it lightly, without any further research or input, or you can delve more deeply and use it in conjunction with your birth chart. You are in control. You can dip in and out or immerse yourself fully. Either way, it will help you to align with the energy of the stars and master the art of living your very best life. And as we each do this, and raise our vibration, we harness the power to help both ourselves and our Divine Mother, the Earth.

Remember these words and keep them in your heart at all times:

> *It only takes one light to illuminate a dark room.*
> *You are that light.*

Using this journal will help you to shine. It will empower you to become your own life coach, maximize your potential and, perhaps, even prevent you from making the mistakes that you can avoid. It will inform you and help you to plan your moves accordingly. Astrology is a report on the energy fields surrounding us. We often react to these according to our own astrology, and so, some basic knowledge of your own birth chart, combined with the information in this journal, will give you an edge and enable you to perfect your sense of timing.

All astrology is subject to interpretation, so I only offer potentials for how certain alignments may play out. But the more you know your own chart (*see page xii*), the more your own insights will flow through. Also, as your personal coach this year, I have designed "missions" to better manage the energy of the coming months and help you raise your awareness, open up your heart and mind to the enlightening rhythms of the universe and increase your physical well-being. You are not obligated to complete any of them, but they will serve as a safety net that is always there to support you, whenever you feel you need it.

So, use this journal in one of three ways:

1. As you would your everyday diary. Read the tips and guidance and note down your thoughts. Oh, and notice the impacts of the Moon phases and astrological movements on your life ...

2. More personally: lean in and use your own birth chart to match the movements of the planets and signs throughout the journal with your chart. That way you will know when the stars and planets are majorly impacting you.

3. Alongside your own birth chart: use the astrological information to go deeper and enhance your everyday life and interactions.

Whichever way you choose, you can't lose! Nobody is judging you.

Ready to dive in?

Remember, awareness is first, then informed action follows! Are you aware of what's in your birth chart?

Your birth chart is a snapshot of the position of certain stars and planets at the moment of your birth. Information is power, and the knowledge and insight that this snapshot provides will enable you to become more empowered. You can find out how to draw your birth chart on page xii.

We all have major planets and a sprinkling of every astrological sign in our birth chart and, with a little know-how, we can figure out not only when and how they are likely to impact us, but also how we can make the most of the star-sent energies to enhance our daily life. Whether you are a barista or ballet dancer, knowing what's going on energetically enables you to choose how and even when to respond.

The path to enlightenment is never easy, but it is always rewarding. There are plenty of tools available to assist you, but it's a journey that ultimately only you can choose to make. Making the commitment to understanding yourself is the first step. So, go on, draw your chart:

- Go to dynamicastrology.com and click on "Chart Calculator," where you may draw your chart for free. If you don't know what time you were born, no worries, just click "Unknown."

We will be working with the planets and signs in this journal, for example the Moon in Libra (as pictured).

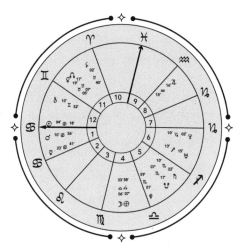

The planets represent "what" – what that means for you. Each planet represents something. For example, the Moon represents "emotional strength," "emotional well-being" and how we "feel" in general.

The signs are "how" – how that plays out for you. It can play out well or not so well, of course. For example, in Libra, "gone right," the Moon indicates "emotional balance, fairness, diplomacy, and a drive to form harmonious relationships," and "gone wrong," it can be "judgmental, desperate for any relationship and vain."

- Click on all the planets, signs, houses and symbols in your chart and on the website and fill in the table on page xvi. I find writing something down helps you to remember it.

- Although the stars' and planets' movements affect us all, certain signs are more impacted than others at differing times, so to make the most of this journal, refer to this table to discover when the astrology of a month, week or day will impact you most. In the journal I also list the signs that are due for a power surge. So, again, check your chart and see when and where the signs' and planets' influence will be intensified. Note that influence can "go right" or "go wrong"; how we handle it is our choice!

# The Planets

### The Sun

We all have our very own Sun in our birth chart. Our Sun sign is the sign that most of us know; it's also known as the star sign. You might like to make a note in your journal of when the actual Sun moves into your sign. This is your time of ultimate strength and potential for brilliance.

### The Moon

We all have our very own Moon in our birth chart. This is useful to know, especially if we wish to manage our moods. It's helpful to make a note in your journal of when the actual Moon is in your sign. It's going to happen every month. This is your time of emotional strength. And if the New or Full Moon falls in your sign, its impact is amplified.

### Mercury

We all have our very own Mercury in our birth chart. This is useful to know, especially if we wish to manage our mind, or negotiations and communications in general. Once you've drawn your chart and know where your planets are, make a note in your journal of when Mercury meets them or is in your sign. This is your time of mental strength and heightened intelligence.

### Venus

We all have our very own Venus in our birth chart. This is useful to know, especially if we wish to enhance our love life and attractiveness. Make a note in your journal of when Venus connects to your other planets or is in your sign. This is your time of charm and attractiveness.

### Mars

We all have our very own Mars in our birth chart. This is useful to know, especially if we wish to manage our overall energy and powers of attraction. Make a note in your journal of when Mars meets your other planets or is in your sign. This is your time of physical energy, power of attraction and drive.

### Jupiter

We all have our very own Jupiter in our birth chart. This is useful to know, especially if we wish to attract good fortune or be aware of when we might go over the top. Knowing when Jupiter meets your other planets, or is in your sign, will ensure that you make the most of your time of abundance and good fortune. Remember that we often only recognize good fortune long after the event!

### Saturn

We all have our very own Saturn in our birth chart. This is useful to know, especially if we wish to master certain aspects of our life or overcome challenges from the past (even past lives). Make a note in your journal of when Saturn connects to your other planets or is in your sign. This is your time of learning, achieving and succeeding through hard work and valuable lessons.

### Uranus

We all have our very own Uranus in our birth chart. This is useful to know, especially if we wish to increase our overall awareness and hone our ability to progress. Make a note in your journal of when Uranus connects to your other planets or is in your sign. This is your time of heightened awareness, power, insight, ideas and ingenuity.

### Neptune

We all have our very own Neptune in our birth chart. This is useful to know, especially if we wish to know what to let go of in order to avoid confusion and illusion, and also how to increase our intuition and heed our dreams. Make a note in your journal of when Neptune connects to your other planets or is in your sign. This is your time of surrender and also time to increase your connection to the spiritual realms.

### Pluto

We all have our very own Pluto in our birth chart. This is useful to know, especially if we wish to know where our power lies or where we may experience the most transformative experiences and attune to our motivation. Make a note in your journal of when Pluto connects with your other planets or is in your sign. This is your time of power and also when your potential for transformation is increased.

### Chiron

We all have our very own Chiron in our birth chart. This is useful to know, especially if we wish to know where our "karmic wound" lies and which area offers the most potential for soul healing. Recognize wounds and pain as the great teachers and opportunities for growth that they are.

### The North Node

We all have our very own North Node in our birth chart. This is useful to know, especially if you wish to know the sign that holds the key to your karmic direction in this life. Make a note in your journal of when the North Node connects to your planets or is in your sign. This is your time of purpose and is also the time to increase your understanding of the most rewarding path for you.

# Your Birth Chart

| MY CHART | | |
|---|---|---|
| **The Planets** | **My Signs** | **My Movements** |
| ☉ Sun | | |
| ☽ Moon | | |
| ☿ Mercury | | |
| ♀ Venus | | |
| ♂ Mars | | |
| ♃ Jupiter | | |
| ♄ Saturn | | |
| ♅ Uranus | | |
| ♆ Neptune | | |
| ♇ Pluto | | |
| ⚷ Chiron | | |
| ☊ North Node | | |

# January

The very first day of the new year begins with some gentle energy, which may have us all feeling a little spaced out or ungrounded. The Moon is in Pisces, so for those of us who chose to spend New Year's Eve on a retreat from the worldly bustle, this is the perfect time for contemplation and spiritual practice, such as deep meditation and Yoga, and for setting clear intentions for the year ahead. For those of us who parted company with 2019 at a party, it may mean we take longer than usual to recover. Whatever you are doing, be kind to yourself and recoup your energy, which will return full flow when Mars switches sign on January 3rd.

## Signs in the Spotlight

 *Capricorn* (also its opposite sign, *Cancer*, to a lesser degree, until the Full Moon in Cancer on January 10th).

 *Aquarius* (also its opposite sign, *Leo*, to a lesser degree).

 *Pisces* (also its opposite sign, *Virgo*, to a lesser degree).

 *Sagittarius* (also its opposite sign, *Gemini*, to a lesser degree).

 *Scorpio* (also its opposite sign, *Taurus*, equally).

# Intentions

If you didn't conjure up an adequately inspiring New Year's resolution list, work on a new one now and release any fears under the Full Moon on January 10th instead – the Full Moon is such a powerful time for purification!

Mars has been in the deep, penetrating sign of Scorpio since November 2019. This is a perfect combination for tenacity on one level and attracting soul mates on another. It's also a time for deepening existing relationships with those who bring out the very best in us, for it's all about chemistry and attraction that goes way beyond the physical. However, while Scorpio energy "gone right" is forgiving, empathetic and extremely powerful, when things aren't going well it's prone to be stuck in the past and playing the blame game. Avoid this trait and set an intention to love yourself and release anything that causes you pain. Self-love is a far cry from narcissism; it's a gentle inner confidence that knows you are already good enough, and are, indeed, the most powerful player in your life, with the potential to transform any area or trait that you no longer wish to work with.

# Reflect, Re-energize

The planets' combinations are pushing us to be serious and driven this month and will offer support to those of us who have solid goals. However, this is matched in power with serious amounts of air and fire, which energize and inspire.

Overall, it's vital for our well-being that we give ourselves regular breaks and take some time off to reflect on anything we need to leave behind. Our energy will be revived by the Great Mother (nature) when Mars moves into adventure-loving Sagittarius on January 3rd. After that, we will be energized by feeding our mind with higher knowledge and becoming more philosophical. Taking walks, surfing waves or hopping on bikes to reconnect with the elements will also reboot our energy and shoot arrows of inspiration our way.

The Aquarian influence this year is eclectic, accelerated and, at times, wild, and so to avoid burnout we must take time out from busy schedules. Our New Year's vows should include being kind to ourselves and spending time with people and animals who heal and nourish our soul.

# Revolution Brings Opportunity

Uranus, the planet that sparks revolution and change, has been in a retrograde motion (appearing to go backward) since August last year, but finally goes direct in Taurus on January 11th. This will enable us to actualize the ideas that have been percolating away for some time; it also pushes us to become more aware of our resources and our body, and how we care for them. Pushing ourselves to extremes is not wise; finding ways to nourish mind, body and soul will set us up to achieve total soul contentment. Roll out your Yoga mat at home or in the office, plan your own class or find a fab teacher online; whatever you do, truly embrace this new year as one in which to find your balance.

This is actually a year that will give us the opportunities to achieve our wildest dreams, but with all the Capricorn vibes at the start of this month – and throughout most of the year, thanks to Saturn and Jupiter – they won't come easily if we haven't worked for them.

If we are prepared to face our shortcomings and put the work in, however, January will allow us to sow seeds that, with care and patience, will flourish just like the stunning biodynamic vineyards producing the finest grapes, all cultivated via the phases of the Moon.

# Empowerment

The Sun shines in a sign for almost one month, magnifying and empowering the energy of that sign. Capricorn energy is magnified until January 20th and then the Sun moves on to empower Aquarius. For now, though, Capricorn energy impacts us all collectively, and the effect is even more powerful for those of us with Capricorn as our Sun sign, Moon sign, rising sign (first house), or any other major "stamp," or its opposite sign, Cancer.

This discerning yet ambitious vibe will affect us all and so we need to make sure we channel the "gone right" vibe: committed, reliable and *über*-wise. The alternative is not very attractive: megalomania, ruthlessness and a calculating approach; think politics gone wrong. Avoid political contests and just remember that hard work and steadfastness always pay off – in one lifetime or another!

For those of you with major stamps in Capricorn (and Cancer, to a lesser degree), this month will enable you to make wise moves, taking the greater goal into consideration, and to impress those in authority – or maybe you'll just impress yourself. With all of the activity in Capricorn, you will no doubt be reviewing changes you wish to make. These may be work-related, personal or spiritual, but try not to be too hard on yourself – another Capricorn trait you own. Accept where you are and know that this year is all about waking up and taking your rightful place as a warrior in a time starred for immense transformation.

Spiritual practice is a must if you are to capitalize on the star movements and chart the territories smoothly.

For you, Capricorn, having Jupiter, Saturn, Pluto and the Sun in your sign is very empowering, but also way too much pressure. So, relax, lighten up and embrace your mantra.

*Capricorn's mantra*: **I am enough.**

# Wednesday, January 1st– Sunday, January 5th

## Forecast

This week begins with Pisces Moon energy possibly causing us to float away with our dreams. In order to gain the most from the astrology this week, and beyond, it's vital that we immerse ourselves in nature and give ourselves some headspace. By the time Mars moves from brooding Scorpio into Sagittarius on January 3rd, we should be feeling ready to shake off the holiday season's lethargy and crack on with goals and activities that inspire us.

Certain aspects square to Pluto push us to open our minds or the minds of others and change the way we perceive certain areas of our lives. And, because it's directly connected to the fixed sign of Taurus, it's better to adopt a patient, gently tenacious approach if we wish to succeed. Taurus energy responds well to a pragmatic attitude, and if you have to handle challenging issues or people, focus on planting seeds slowly and then letting go of the need to see immediate results.

If it's you that is fixed, then you need to be more patient with yourself; this life is like a drop in the ocean, but one that still causes ripples, and even the smallest step toward a goal or change will undoubtedly get results.

## Mission

- Ten minutes of morning meditation each day. You may use an app or any other tool to assist you; however, the real goal here is to just sit quietly with your mind and make friends with it. Set an alarm for ten minutes (or more if you wish) and try to always sit in the same place at the same time with your sitting position well aligned. Try not to move, and when a thought comes (and they do!), don't chase it, just accept it and let it go and then return to deep breaths. In life we often make moves to chase pleasure and avert suffering. When we train the mind to remain unmoved, it's a serious game changer, as the mind creates our reality.

● In Greek, *meraki* is the word that defines anything that you create with all of your heart and pure soul. Direct *meraki* into all that you do this week. Inject your heart, soul and creativity into simple tasks and projects.

*Aspiration/mantra*: **Patience.**

# Wednesday, January 1st

**New Year's Day.**
The Moon is in Pisces. This is a great time for imagination and romance. The energy may be a little spacey, so use this time to recover with gentle and uplifting people and pastimes, or to meditate and activate the higher vision and third-eye chakra.

**Mission completed?** Challenge level: 1–5: Ideas and insights:

_____

_____

# Thursday, January 2nd

The Moon moves into Aries. There is more emotional energy available, which can be directed toward self-care and personal plans.
Power surge for those with Aries stamps.

**Mission completed?** Challenge level: 1–5: Ideas and insights:

_____

_____

## Friday, January 3rd

Mars enters Sagittarius. There is more inspirational energy available for us to use. If you are failing to feel the shift, take time out in nature, and any time you feel less than positive, repeat: "I attract inspiration."
Power surge for those with Sagittarius stamps.

**Mission completed?** Challenge level: 1–5: Ideas and insights:

## Saturday, January 4th

The Moon moves into Taurus. This is a fabulous time to focus on nourishment. Maybe avoid shopping sprees and do something that nourishes your soul: cook a healthy meal from scratch for some friends (without using any animal products) and see how you feel. Perhaps even research a "bad-karma-free" recipe! Direct *meraki* into all you do. Other people really will feel it!

**Mission completed?** Challenge level: 1–5: Ideas and insights:

## Sunday, January 5th

**Mission completed?** Challenge level: 1–5: Ideas and insights:

# Reflections ...

If you managed to complete this week's mission, how did it make you feel?

If you skipped anything, did you feel any different?

Did you notice whether the Moon phases or Mars's shift made you do anything differently or feel different?

How did the week's aspiration unfold? Did it help you to cultivate patience or become aware of when you, or another, lacked in it?

List a few things, or even just one, that you are grateful for. This is a powerful indicator to the universe that you are aware of its blessings.

Are there any takeaways from this week that you would like to address next week? Try reflecting without judgment.

# Monday, January 6th– Sunday, January 12th

## Forecast

This week we have a major Full Moon impacting us and also a lunar eclipse in the sign of Cancer, which is doubly powerful as the Moon is the ruler of Cancer. Cancer is all about emotions and how we feel in general. Back in old England, citing lunacy for crimes committed under a Full Moon was a strong defence, and people who lost their minds were branded "lunatics." Now the Moon's phases are known to cause a gravitational pull upon large bodies of water, and humans are comprised of around 65 per cent water, so it stands to reason that the Full Moon is going to impact us mortals as well as the tides. Given that we have this knowledge, let's hold it together and use our wisdom to transform any explosive energy into calmness and tolerance. Don't get sucked into reacting when others do. Take three deep breaths and pump compassion into the planet. If we all do this under the Full Moon, we will steady the Earth's vibrations, vanquish demons and win many karmic points this month. I like winning and I'm a team player, so let's do this collectively. It's all about the "Om" – chant it, calm down and focus on compassion ...

Uranus breaks out of its retrograde funk this week and starts working for us again, which is rather marvelous, and it aligns with the sign of Taurus, the latter being Mother Earth's official guardian, so if we take our carbon footprint into account and tone down our consumeristic ways, then Uranus, the god of the skies, and his mythic wife, Gaia, will stand by us and bestow many blessings.

# Mission

In addition to ten minutes of morning meditation, prepare for the emotional impact of the Full Moon by releasing stagnant energy with simple Yoga moves:

- Sit cross-legged on the floor with a straight back and place your hands gently on your knees.
- Ground yourself with the floor and gently extend your spine as you inhale. Imagine light flooding through the crown of your head.
- With your eyes closed, take deep breaths through your nose and fill your lungs with oxygen. Pause and hold your breath for a few seconds.
- Slowly exhale all of the air from your lungs through your nose, creating a gentle "oceanic" sound in the back of your throat.
- Repeat this practice for two to three minutes.

*Aspiration/mantra*: **Let it go!**

## Monday, January 6th

Today is likely to be fast-paced, so take time out and try not to overcommit, in order to avoid stress and burnout.
Power surge for those with Gemini stamps.

**Mission completed?** Challenge level: 1–5: Ideas and insights:

## Tuesday, January 7th

The Moon moves into Gemini.

**Mission completed?** Challenge level: 1–5: Ideas and insights:

---

## Wednesday, January 8th

Rather lovely energy around today, so pump out love and kindness. Avoid unrealistic expectations and stay present.
Power surge for those with Cancer stamps.

**Mission completed?** Challenge level: 1–5: Ideas and insights:

---

## Thursday, January 9th

The Moon moves into Cancer.

**Mission completed?** Challenge level: 1–5: Ideas and insights:

# Friday, January 10th

Power surge for those with Leo stamps.

## Full Moon in Cancer (2:21 pm EST)

The Full Moon is the time to release and let go of any habits, people or situations that don't serve our hearts, minds or higher purpose. Also, this Full Moon will go through what's known as an "appulse" eclipse, when the Moon is obscured by the Earth's shadow. It is this lack of light that, perhaps, awakens us and allows us to recognize our own shadow side. I believe that there is no more powerful time to face our demons and, in doing so, release them to the light.

In days gone by, when we were all God-fearing people, eclipses were seen as bad omens. They are extremely powerful and, for this reason, monks in many Buddhist monasteries in the East take vows of silence at this time, believing that the karma is magnified under the Full Moon; they pray and meditate for world peace.

- Write down all of the aspects of yourself, or your life, that you wish to release, such as "I want to release: my anxiety, my aversion to fitness, toxic relationships." You can ask the Moon Goddess to help you to surrender, release and move on!

- Burn your list (safely) under the magnificent force of the Full Moon. Ask for help from the unseen forces; have faith, trust that all is well and know that there is an underlying plan.

This will be a double impact, as the Moon governs the sign of Cancer. Watch out for people overreacting today; stay calm, calm others and breathe deeply. You have the power to transform this energy into empathy, affinity and great kindness. Because you have the knowledge!

**Mission completed?** Challenge level: 1–5: Ideas and insights:

---

---

# Saturday, January 11th

The Moon moves into Leo.
Uranus goes direct in Taurus.
Power surge for those with Aquarius, Leo and Taurus stamps.

**Mission completed?** Challenge level: 1–5: Ideas and insights:

---

---

# Sunday, January 12th

Saturn forms an exact conjunction to Pluto in Capricorn today, causing an extraordinary energy surge for us all. You may feel the need to reassess your goals and commitments in life, but this surge is more geared toward Capricorn and, to a lesser degree, Scorpio. Both planets trigger the need for profound transformation and rebirth. To be able to do this smoothly, forgive, forget and find new ways to operate.

**Mission completed?** Challenge level: 1–5: Ideas and insights:

---

---

# Reflections ...

If you managed to complete this week's mission, how did it make you feel?

If you skipped anything, did you feel any different?

Did the Full Moon impact you?

How did the week's aspiration unfold? Did it help you to remember to breathe more, or become aware of when you, or another, overreacted?

List a few things, or even just one, that you are grateful for.

Are there any takeaways from this week that you would like to address next week? Try reflecting without judgment.

# Monday, January 13th–Sunday, January 19th

## Forecast

Mercury moves into Aquarius this week, ushering in powerful, high-vibrational and exhilarating energy.

The best use of the week is to align with the higher mind, as Aquarius is working steadfastly for the shift in consciousness, sending sacred wisdom to remind us of who we really are. These cosmic downloads lift us out of a purely worldly existence and help us to realign with the collective consciousness and, indeed, our true selves. Busy minds cannot capture the above, though. When your phone's memory or computer's hard drive is full, it simply cannot receive or retain any new information, and it's the same with your mind. So, if you wish to attune to, hear, feel and use the knowledge provided by Aquarius, spend time alone, meditate daily and do not get caught up in trivia. Although the week is likely to be busy and brimming with exciting opportunities, allow yourself some freedom from the rat race and time to be quiet.

Uranus, the ruler of Aquarius, is flowing forward and because it's in the earth sign Taurus we need to steady its electric flashes and keep our feet on the ground. I've said this before, but daily meditation and Yoga, or perhaps *Qi Gong*, will protect you and keep you in tune with your mind, body and soul. Uranus is the master of the unexpected and likes to send surprises that invigorate and cause shocks of electric energy. Being steady will protect you and help you enjoy the opportunities for learning that the week ahead will provide.

In addition, Venus moves into Pisces, which is a sensitive, gentle and mellow sign at its best. Pisces "gone right" sees clearly, avoids toxins, including alcohol, and stays present in the wonder of the moment. So, this can be an amazing week for creative expression. To avoid Virgo "gone wrong," which potentially impacts at the beginning of the week and heightens anxiety, a total clear-out is advised. Prepare for the week ahead as much as you possibly can and, on a practical level, arrange your work and home space in order to "feel" organized. Go through paperwork, pay bills and recycle. Venus shifting into Pisces on Monday lightens up the Virgo vibe, but it's prudent to heed the above before allowing Pisces "gone right" to flood the senses with feel-good juices: play music, make art, manage the mind with meditation and Yoga, and go with the flow of life.

# Mission

In addition to ten minutes of morning meditation, it's important to detoxify, to prepare and open your mind to receive, so try to avoid alcohol or any other mind-altering substances for the next week and sleep without interference. If you have a busy family life, maybe recruit the family and ask them to support you as you find new ways to better manage everyday life. If you do include them, ask them to add their own reflections to your journal. If the children are little, simply ask them how they feel afterward and how they dream. His Holiness the Dalai Lama once said, "If every eight-year-old in the world is taught meditation, we will eliminate violence from the world within one generation."

Our subconscious often works through our conscious mind and through dreams, so keep your mind clear to create space. At bedtime for the next five days at least (seven if you can!), enact the following ritual and create your own safe and sacred sleeping space:

- Remove or switch off any electrical items.

- Light some candles or burn some incense.

- Sit cross-legged, palms facing upward on your knees. Close your eyes and take several deep breaths. Repeat in your mind: "I am open to receiving through my dreams."

Remember to blow out the candles before you sleep!

*Aspiration/mantra:* **I am open to receiving.**

# Monday, January 13th

The Moon moves into Virgo.
Venus moves into Pisces. Avoid criticism and, wherever possible, side-step anyone who is anything other than kind today: smile and detach graciously. Power surge for those with Virgo and Pisces stamps.

**Mission completed?** Challenge level: 1–5: Ideas and insights:

---

---

# Tuesday, January 14th

**Mission completed?** Challenge level: 1–5: Ideas and insights:

---

---

# Wednesday, January 15th

The Moon moves into Libra. There is a wonderful connection to Mercury today, helping to magnify the "gone right" traits of Libra. Communications should be free flowing and harmonious, and an air of goodwill should surround us. Avoid superficial glamor and embrace the true beauty that exists within.
Power surge for Libra and Taurus.

**Mission completed?** Challenge level: 1–5: Ideas and insights:

---

---

## Thursday, January 16th

Mercury enters Aquarius.
Power surge for those with major stamps in Aquarius or Gemini.

**Mission completed?** Challenge level: 1–5: Ideas and insights:

## Friday, January 17th

The Moon moves into Scorpio. Intense feelings and energies surround us right now, so let go of low vibes and negative thinking and switch to feelings of optimism, unity and empathy.

**Mission completed?** Challenge level: 1–5: Ideas and insights:

## Saturday, January 18th

**Mission completed?** Challenge level: 1–5: Ideas and insights:

## Sunday, January 19th

**Mission completed?** Challenge level: 1–5: Ideas and insights:

# Reflections ...

If you managed to complete this week's mission, how did it make you feel?

_____

_____

If you skipped anything, did you feel any different?

_____

_____

How did the week's aspiration unfold?

_____

_____

Did you feel any different in the mornings after your evening rituals?

_____

_____

List a few things, or even just one, that you are grateful for.

_____

_____

Are there any takeaways from this week that you would like to address next week? Try reflecting without judgment.

_____

_____

# Monday, January 20th–Sunday, January 26th

## Forecast

The Sun moves into Aquarius, which is exciting, and provides some seriously eclectic situations and random happenings, which are always fun! The star-sent energy this week also provides an abundance of mental stimulation. As with any Aquarian power surges, we need to take time out to recharge, though, or else run the genuine risk of short-circuiting!

This week is brimming with fire and air, and this is a winning combination when channeled into creativity or connecting the subtle dots that less tuned-in beings simply fail to see.

The Sun connects to Mercury in Aquarius, and so opportunities to socialize and network with influential and like-minded people will no doubt present themselves. The people we meet under this astrological influence are very likely to be valuable, with a role to play in the spiritual revolution, so keep an open heart and mind, yet remain discerning.

Mars and the Moon connect in Sagittarius, which encourages us to travel and seek "off the beaten track" experiences. If you cannot escape to faraway lands, work with what you have, satiating Mars and the Moon in Sagittarius's thirst for adventure with higher knowledge. Seek out a real spiritual teacher or read some inspiring books and spiritual texts.

The Moon connects to Jupiter in Capricorn, so this sign's impact is trebled in power and will probably cause some of us to work hard and take everything rather seriously. This can be a good time if we need to stay focused and determined.

After this, the New Moon in Aquarius gives us fantastic abilities to manifest opportunity and magic for the future.

# Mission

In addition to ten minutes of morning meditation, which will help you to stay grounded in the midst of the Aquarian chaos, let's work on receptivity and training your intuition to serve you better. Your intuition is like a muscle, so the more you train it, the stronger it becomes. If you master the following exercise, you can use it to "tune in" to your intuition faster than the blink of an eye!

- Each morning, while you are fresh (i.e., before you look at your phone!), add the following exercise into your morning routine:

  ○ Find a place to sit comfortably without slouching. Close your eyes.

  ○ Take deep breaths by counting "one" on the inhale and "two" on the exhale, always with your mouth closed, breathing through your nose.

  ○ When you are relaxed and still, identify an event or situation that you'd like more insight about.

  ○ Keep breathing deeply. (This prevents the naughty ego-mind telling you what works best for it!)

  ○ Ask a question about the event or situation you wish to gain insight into. Make it a simple question initially, with a "yes" or "no" answer.

  ○ Keep breathing deeply! The answer should come within a second, either as a fleeting feeling or as a straight verbal answer.

Practice makes perfect!

*Aspiration/mantra:* **We are all connected.**

# Monday, January 20th

The Sun enters Aquarius.
The Moon moves into Sagittarius.

**Mission completed?** Challenge level: 1–5: Ideas and insights:

---

# Tuesday, January 21st

Neptune is working on us all but is particularly poignant for those with major Capricorn stamps, so be gentle and appreciative of yourself and others. Stay positive and speak kindly to yourself.

**Mission completed?** Challenge level: 1–5: Ideas and insights:

---

# Wednesday, January 22nd

The Moon moves into Capricorn.

**Mission completed?** Challenge level: 1–5: Ideas and insights:

---

# Thursday, January 23rd

**Mission completed?** Challenge level: 1–5: Ideas and insights:

# Friday, January 24th

## New Moon in Aquarius (4:42 PM EST)

The most fertile time to plant seeds for change this month will be under the phase of the New Moon, as this is the perfect time to set out your intentions for the future:

- Before you conjure up your New Moon intention list for the month ahead, though, it would be wise to meditate and perhaps roll out the Yoga mat to release the stagnant *dukka* (bad energy) to help you to gain fresh perspective and insight. It's better to avoid self-serving desires and instead work with the higher mind toward an inclusive goal that will benefit others as well. Humanity is well starred to unite as never before in this Aquarian Age; it's healing for our heart and important for the revolution that we do our bit! So, align with your higher mind and manifest the magic!

- It's best to burn your list at the time of the New Moon, but it is potent all day, so don't worry if you are late.

Strong energy is available in abundance this month, so don't miss the waves of awareness. Surf them!

**Mission completed?** Challenge level: 1–5: Ideas and insights:

## Saturday, January 25th

Power surge for those with major stamps in Gemini or Pisces.

**Mission completed?** Challenge level: 1–5: Ideas and insights:

_____

_____

## Sunday, January 26th

**Mission completed?** Challenge level: 1–5: Ideas and insights:

_____

_____

# Reflections ...

If you managed to complete this week's mission, how did it make you feel?

_____

_____

If you skipped anything, did you feel any different?

_____

_____

Did you feel a change in energy this week?

Did the New Moon impact you? Or those around you?

How did the week's aspiration unfold?

List a few things, or even just one, that you are grateful for.

Are there any takeaways from this week that you would like to address next week? Try reflecting without judgment.

# Monday, January 27th– Friday, January 31st

## Forecast

This is the final week of the first month of 2020! And however you have chosen to use your journal, it's likely to have had a positive impact. Even a fleeting "aha" moment brought about by simply knowing when the Moon is in your sign is helpful. The Moon connects to Venus, in Pisces, at the beginning of this week. This is not usually the most productive energy when actualizing, or solidifying, agreements and plans. Channeling your inner artist (we do all have one!) is likely to deliver more satisfying results.

Imagination and overall perception is magnified at this time, and if you can keep your mind pure, you will avoid the feelings of loss, disillusionment or confusion often sent by Pisces "gone wrong." Playing beautiful music, or even writing your own, is well starred. Taking time out from the relentless schedule of everyday life is also way more productive than becoming frustrated when plans go awry or when people flake out on you. Accept, try to let go of the need to control, and make the most of this time by conjuring up fresh visions and allowing the universe to take charge. Trust is the key: get out of the driver's seat and become a passenger this week, allowing cool, artistic and deeply spiritual Pisces to rule the show.

## Mission

- Ten minutes of morning meditation each day, which will increase your ability to tune in to the subtle whispers of the universe and guide you toward your soul's wisdom.

- This week it's all about awakening your own inner artist and amplifying the compassion in your life, so:

○ Say something kind to yourself in the mirror every morning and night, as you brush your teeth. Look into your eyes and reconnect with your soul. Make friends with yourself.

○ Pause before you say anything negative to yourself, or another person. Stop the words and release them from your mind.

○ Visit a new art exhibition, even if you have never been to one before. Allow the art to speak to you. Art is always divinely inspired, even though it evokes different feelings in us all.

○ Buy some fresh flowers for your home or workspace and arrange them beautifully.

*Aspiration/mantra*: **Trust.**

# Monday, January 27th

The Moon moves into Pisces.

**Mission completed?** Challenge level: 1–5: Ideas and insights:

_____

_____

# Tuesday, January 28th

**Mission completed?** Challenge level: 1–5: Ideas and insights:

_____

_____

## Wednesday, January 29th

The Moon moves into Aries.
Power surge for those with major stamps in Aries and, to a lesser degree, Libra.

**Mission completed?** Challenge level: 1–5: Ideas and insights:

---

## Thursday, January 30th

**Mission completed?** Challenge level: 1–5: Ideas and insights:

---

## Friday, January 31st

Carry out at least one random act of kindness (without telling another soul about it) and pop it into your reflections at the end of this week. Note how you feel about your good little secret deed.

**Mission completed?** Challenge level: 1–5: Ideas and insights:

---

# Reflections ...

If you managed to complete this week's mission, how did it make you feel?

---

If you skipped anything, did you feel any different?

_____

_____

Did you carry out a secret act of kindness? What triggered this and how did it make you feel?

_____

_____

How did the week's aspiration unfold?

_____

_____

List a few things, or even just one, that you are grateful for.

_____

_____

Are there any takeaways from this week that you would like to address next week? Try reflecting without judgment.

_____

_____

Now relax. Relax before you turn the page to February. Be in the moment! Make some notes and give yourself a gold star for the missions that you completed throughout the month.

_____

_____

# February

Welcome to February, which is a leap month. This means that 2020 is a leap year! Leap years are required to keep our calendar in sync. They date back to 45 BC, when Julius Caesar's calendar reforms were put into practice. The twelve months of his Julian calendar had thirty and thirty-one days, apart from February, which had twenty-eight. However, when Augustus succeeded Julius as Caesar, the Roman Senate changed the name of the eighth month to August in his honor and because his predecessor's month, July, had thirty-one days and August only had thirty, they took a day from February to equalize it. How beneficial for Augustus this was we may never know, but we do know that he died in his "own" month! The calendar was still flawed, but it wasn't until 1,500 years later that Pope Gregory changed it to the Gregorian calendar we use today.

In numerology, a leap year is known as a number two and number eleven (second month: 2, twenty-ninth day: 2 + 9 = 11) time. The number two is often described as the stoic and powerful female who bows her head, displaying humility, but never breaks or fails to exercise grace. The number eleven is the first "master number," hence this is a time of heightened intuition, spiritual power and supernatural abilities. The number two is associated (not unnaturally) with the second sign of the zodiac, Taurus, which is associated with grace, beauty and resilience. Eleven is also associated with the eleventh sign of the zodiac, Aquarius, the sign responsible for the awakening of humanity and general shift in consciousness.

Aquarius remains the key player for us all until February 19th, when the Sun shifts into Pisces. This means that the serious vibe lightens for a few weeks and we should enjoy all that the exciting and enlightening influence of this month's stars. It is Aquarius season after all, and this aware and analytical sign's energy is boosted a hundredfold by the connections between the Sun and Mercury. These genius vibes are lightning fast, and we need to be ready to catch them. If we don't note the ideas that these flashes of inspiration trigger, we run the risk of forgetting them. These flashes will affect us all, and so we need to make sure that we channel the "gone right" traits of Aquarius and are compassionate, innovative and wide awake.

Meanwhile Venus is in Pisces at the beginning of the month, which is simply magical for romance and love but not so hot for closing deals and negotiating, as people tend to be on differing planets.

## Signs in the Spotlight

 *Aquarius* (also its opposite sign, *Leo*, to a lesser degree, until the Full Moon in Leo on 9th February).

 *Pisces* (also its opposite sign, *Virgo*, to a lesser degree).

 *Aries* (also its opposite sign, *Libra*, to a lesser degree).

 *Sagittarius* (also its opposite sign, *Gemini*, to a lesser degree).

## Ground the Body, Steady the Mind

At the start of the month we need to seek stimuli, connect with other people, explore and steady the higher mind with meditation and other practices to help us center and ground our physical body and also calm and steady our mind enough to align with our intuition.

Making the most out of this energy is a wise move; burning ourselves out is not. Accept as many invitations to go out and socialize as you can at the beginning of the month but remember to take time out for spiritual practice and to check in with your soul. You can take control and host dinner parties and gatherings of your own, if you prefer. Go with whatever emerges, and then, when you connect with people who are like-minded, watch the sparks fly!

# Gentle, Spiritual and Artistic

Mercury moves into Pisces on February 3rd, and this is a wonderful energy for imagination, gentleness, spiritual practice and higher vision. We may long to become one with the universe under this influence, which is magical if we associate with productive people and positive endeavors; it's also great for making art, listening to soothing music (or writing our own) and for indulging the artist that resides within all of us.

It's probably a good move to retreat for a few days at this time in order to reflect, as we are likely to be more sensitive than ever. So, walk on the beach or in the park or climb a mountain and meditate at the top. It's not such a wise move to seek escape routes through associations with toxic people or substances that are negatively mind-altering, like alcohol or drugs.

# Solutions and Vision

By the time Venus shifts into Aries on February 7th, we can happily begin to make plans that are likely to solidify. Aries energy is dynamic but can be impatient, forceful even, and, if we are not careful, we run the risk of being perceived as aggressive. Venus in Aries can be superb, though, when combined with Pisces and Aquarius. Pisces inspires the vision, Aquarius offers genius solutions and can see the bigger picture, and Aries knows how to motivate and get s%*t done!

# Mercury Retrograde

The Sun moves to connect with the graceful sign of Pisces on February 19th, and Mercury goes retrograde in Pisces on February 17th, remaining so until March 10th. Although this will not stop progress, it often prevents plans from panning out precisely as we anticipate, so it's far more effective to simply do what we can and then let go, go with the flow and trust in our subtle higher mind and the rhythms of the universe. I do not subscribe to the cult of "fearmongering" that sweeps through the nation under the Mercury retrograde phases. Years ago, when we were more superstitious and less informed, when those who studied the stars saw what appeared to be planets going backward, they took this to be a bad omen: a planet was changing its motion and running away from Earth, seemingly abandoning ship!

We are now educated enough to realize that a retrograde is not a planet running away from us after all, it's simply an optical illusion, and, from an astrological stance and my own experience, it pumps out energy that is neither positive nor negative, just different. You shouldn't pay any attention to the superstition that says it's "bad" – that is not logical. Astrological awareness, when combined with logic (astro + logic), forms a powerful everyday tool, one that enhances life and deepens interactions.

So, don't fall victim to astro gossip and low-vibe/old-fashioned fearmongering about what you should and should not do when Mercury is retrograde. The stars just shine; they pump out energy that can be used or misused and it is up to us how we interpret it.

Mars, the planet/god of war and action, switches sign on February 16th to join Capricorn. This is likely to invigorate our professional needs and overall ambitions, and we are likely to sidestep the idealistic distractions sent by Aquarius and Pisces and get back to revisiting and revising our New Year's intentions.

*Aquarius's mantra*: **I am special.**

# Saturday, February 1st– Sunday, February 2nd

## Forecast

This weekend begins with the Sun in Aquarius, pushing us to attune with our higher mind and to conjure up concepts that serve humanity and the planet. This is magnified for those with the Sun and other strong stamps in the sign but impacts us all and may wake us up to the connections we have in our life and lead us to consider which to nurture and which to leave behind.

Be sure to get enough rest and sleep over the weekend, as the planets are sure to be pelting information at us all week; unplug for long enough to heal from the constant bombardment. Avoid travel this weekend, if you can, and walk or cycle to your destinations. Walk in the park if there's one locally.

## Mission

- At least ten minutes of morning meditation each day is essential in order to help you to relax and heal the mind, body and soul. Create a quiet space to sit either alone or with your partner, family or friends. Set an alarm for ten to fifteen minutes and gently focus on the inhalation and exhalation of breath.

- The Moon is in Taurus until Monday, so it's a great time to connect with the Divine Mother and nourish yourself, and your loved ones, with simple pleasures. It is also prime time to check in with the body, so find a free online *Qi Gong* or Yoga tutorial and flow with it for twenty minutes on both days.

- Prepare home-cooked healthy food and share it. You may even wish to bake your own bread and break it with loved ones.

*Aspiration/mantra*: **Be present.**

## Saturday, February 1st

The Moon is in Taurus.

**Mission completed?** Challenge level: 1–5: Ideas and insights:

_____

_____

## Sunday, February 2nd

**Mission completed?** Challenge level: 1–5: Ideas and insights:

_____

_____

# Reflections ...

If you managed to complete this weekend's mission, how did it make you feel?

_____

_____

If you skipped anything, did you feel any different?

_____

_____

Did you notice the impact of the Sun and Mercury in Aquarius?

_____

_____

Did you feel the nourishing vibes of the Taurus Moon?

How did the weekend's aspiration unfold?

List a few things, or even just one, that you are grateful for.

Are there any takeaways from this weekend that you would like to address next week? Try reflecting without judgment.

# Monday, February 3rd– Sunday, February 9th

## Forecast

The sign of Aquarius evokes an energy, both collectively and individually, that is humanitarian, random, unique and seriously plugged in. Even its ruler, Uranus, has an eccentric orbit in comparison to the other planets; its influence is surprising and innovative but, at worst, shocking. So, insights abound this week, especially as the Sun and Mercury, which governs the individual and collective mind, are in the same sign.

*Take a notebook (or your journal) with you everywhere and jot down ideas and insights that spark this week, for they are sure to be divinely inspired.*

It's important to be present and stay in the moment during this time, as jumping too far ahead can cause unnecessary anxiety.

By the time Venus shifts into Aries on Friday, you may become competitive, or else experience competitive vibes. Do not engage or get impatient; try to exert patience and hold your tongue before any fire-breath scorches hearts.

There is likely to be an excess of electric energy around this week, so be careful that you don't short-circuit or electrocute the people you connect with; slow down, keep a cool head and be sure to get enough rest.

The Full Moon is in Leo on Sunday, so ponder on what you need to release in order to be happier and content in the knowledge that your own soul will always wrap you in love and acceptance.

# Mission

- Ten minutes of meditation each morning is essential to protect the mind under this week's influences.

- In addition to this, it's wise to avoid as much external stimulation as possible before you get caught up in your day. So, break the habit (if you have it) of looking at your phone as soon as you wake up and last thing at night. As soon as you turn on your phone, you are swept into the digital world, and your mission this week is to stay present and steady. Insight and intuition are subtle and refuse to compete with Earthly trivia and distractions. So, ignore your phone until you have done your morning meditation. Start with the chant "Om" and close with three "Oms."

- Repeat the following affirmation daily: "Today is a day brimming with opportunity."

*Aspiration/mantra*: **Slow and steady accomplishments. I create my own happiness.**

## Monday, February 3rd

The Moon moves into Gemini.
Mercury moves into Pisces.
Power surge for those with major stamps in Gemini and Pisces.

**Mission completed?** Challenge level: 1–5: Ideas and insights:

## Tuesday, February 4th

**Mission completed?** Challenge level: 1–5: Ideas and insights:

## Wednesday, February 5th

The Moon moves into Cancer.
Power surge for those with major stamps in Libra and Cancer.

**Mission completed?** Challenge level: 1–5: Ideas and insights:

## Thursday, February 6th

**Mission completed?** Challenge level: 1–5: Ideas and insights:

## Friday, February 7th

The Moon moves into Leo.
Venus moves into Aries.
Power surge for those with major stamps in Aries, Libra, Aquarius, Capricorn and Leo.

**Mission completed?** Challenge level: 1–5: Ideas and insights:

# Saturday, February 8th

**Mission completed?** Challenge level: 1–5: Ideas and insights:

# Sunday, 9th February

## Full Moon in Leo (2:33 AM EST)

The Full Moon is the time to release and let go of those things that no longer serve us; this Full Moon is opposite the Sun in Aquarius. It is pushing us to leave behind self-serving, selfish tendencies in ourselves or those around us and also to let go of the notion that anything other than love and authenticity can make us happy in the long term. The universe is aligned to our soul, and both are in control, so it's better to accept that and to release any superficial relationships or purely worldly desires, as these will not help us.

When we face our fears and let go of our pride, the universe will guide us in return. To access this guidance:

- Make a list of all that you wish to release.
- Contemplate this list before burning it (safely) under the Full Moon.

Power surge for those with major Aquarius, Leo, Aries, Sagittarius and Virgo stamps.

**Mission completed?** Challenge level: 1–5: Ideas and insights:

# Reflections ...

If you managed to complete this week's mission, how did it make you feel?

_____

_____

If you skipped any, did you feel any different?

_____

_____

Did you notice Venus's shift from the water sign, Pisces, into fiery Aries?

_____

_____

Did you feel the effects of the Full Moon? And, if you wrote a Full Moon release list, how did you feel?

_____

_____

List a few things, or even just one, that you are grateful for.

_____

_____

Are there any takeaways from this week that you would like to address next week? Try reflecting without judgment.

_____

_____

# Monday, February 10th– Sunday, February 16th

## Forecast

After the release of the Full Moon, this week will be perfect for planning; you may now begin to set out your intentions for the rest of the month. Don't be too ambitious: Venus in Aries may push you to compare your progress, and indeed life, with that of others, which isn't beneficial, as there will always be people who seem to be more successful or accomplished than we are.

When the Moon shifts into Libra, on Wednesday, we may become judgmental, or otherwise face unfair judgment from others. It is prudent to remember that all that we are, and have, is down to our own karma. Whatever we have, we have already, at some point in our countless existences, earned. It's also sensible to understand that if we are facing challenges, it doesn't mean that we are, or were, a "bad" person, it simply means that we have opportunities to learn and become better versions of ourselves.

This life is precious, but only one of many, and our journey through it is designed to enable the growth of our soul. We can change our karma by becoming more aware of our thoughts, words and actions.

This month is likely to be a reflective one and stopping for a moment to appreciate all that you have will be nourishing. Follow the example of nature: no matter where a flower or tree may be, it always grows toward the light.

This week is possibly going to be an intense one, taking into consideration the Moon's shift into Scorpio on Friday and Mars's shift into Capricorn on Sunday, which bolsters Saturn and Pluto's powers; they can all be rather somber and serious when they get together, so be a rebel with a worthy cause, seek out fun and humor wherever you can, and definitely don't succumb to the authoritarian vibe of the planets pushing you to be serious.

# Mission

Meditate for at least ten minutes every morning in order to strengthen and protect the mind.

In addition to this, your mission this week is to keep your serotonin levels high, especially after Friday's shift in energy. I would suggest at least five minutes of Sun salutations after your sitting meditation practice. This will energize your body, mind and soul and also act as a superb heart-opener. We spend much time in what is known as the "sagittal" plane, bent over desks, phones, steering wheels and the like, that it can result in our hearts closing. For this reason, every day after your meditation, use the following simple techniques to open your heart, boost confidence and increase a sense of joy:

- Create a suitable tranquil space at home, or in the office.
- Sit cross-legged or stand in mountain pose on a mat. Either way, elongate the spine.
- Close your eyes and tune in to your breath, which should be deep and energizing. Let your breath control your movements so that you begin to flow.
- Place your hands on either side of your body, in a "cactus" position. Inhale and then, as you exhale, gently lean back, visualizing your heart opening.
- Inhale and reach up with your arms as if embracing the Sun, looking up at your thumbs. Exhale, lean back slightly and return your arms to the "cactus" position.
- Repeat slowly at a controlled pace.

*Aspiration/mantra:* **I take life sincerely, but never too seriously.**

## Monday, February 10th

The Moon moves into Virgo. This combination may cause anxiety. Do not avert this feeling, for that only magnifies it. Stop, center yourself and breathe deeply. Flood yourself with what I call "feel-good juices." Go back to the basics and tell yourself: "All is well. I am safe. I am protected."
A word on Virgo: it's worth being as organized as you can possibly be during this planetary phase. Go through all of your paperwork, clear out drawers and work to clear your space in order to leave yourself free enough to be creative.

**Mission completed?** Challenge level: 1–5: Ideas and insights:

## Tuesday, February 11th

Power surge for those with stamps in Aries, Sagittarius and Libra.

**Mission completed?** Challenge level: 1–5: Ideas and insights:

## Wednesday, February 12th

The Moon moves into Libra. Adopting an attitude of compromise and diplomacy is advised today. Taking everyone's needs, including your own, into consideration will enable peace and harmony to flow and feelings of justice to prevail.

**Mission completed?** Challenge level: 1–5: Ideas and insights:

# Thursday, February 13th

Power surge for those with stamps in Aries, Sagittarius and Scorpio.

**Mission completed?** Challenge level: 1–5: Ideas and insights:

---

# Friday, February 14th

**Valentine's Day.**
The Moon moves into Scorpio. The general mood is intense and can be directed toward passion. If you are already in a relationship, try to spend time reigniting the joy and affection between you. If you are single, set the intention to feel self-love and appreciation for all that you are.

**Mission completed?** Challenge level: 1–5: Ideas and insights:

---

# Saturday, February 15th

Power surge for those with major stamps in Capricorn and Sagittarius.

**Mission completed?** Challenge level: 1–5: Ideas and insights:

## Sunday, February 16th

The Moon moves into Sagittarius.
Mars moves into Capricorn. Go outside into nature in order to rejuvenate your spirit. Turn your phone off and be in the moment with the divine Mother Earth.

**Mission completed?** Challenge level: 1-5: Ideas and insights:

_____

_____

# Reflections ...

If you managed to complete this week's mission, how did it make you feel?

_____

_____

If you skipped anything, did you feel any different?

_____

_____

Did you feel the effects of the Scorpio Moon this week?

_____

_____

Did you notice the shift in energy, on Sunday, when Mars moved into Capricorn?

_____

_____

Did you manage to spend time outside with your phone switched off?

List a few things, or even just one, that you are grateful for.

Are there any takeaways from this week that you would like to address next week? Try reflecting without judgment.

# Monday, February 17th– Sunday, February 23rd

## Forecast

This week has a rather serious undertone, thanks to Mars, Jupiter and Pluto in Capricorn. This energy is brilliant for focus and general accomplishment. However, there is a catch! Mercury goes retrograde on Monday in Pisces, where it remains until March, then the Sun moves to boost the Pisces vibe on Wednesday too. Pisces and Capricorn are not exactly the best of buddies; that is not to say that they can never be, it's just that they have slightly differing agendas. Pisces likes to go with the flow, follow signs, conjure up visions, create art and dance under the moonlight; Capricorn prefers to control the flow, and prefers road signs to spiritual ones. It's wise to align with the "gone right" traits of Pisces while keeping Capricorn happy, too, and here are my suggestions: avoid anything that alters the state of your consciousness or serves as an anesthetic to the higher mind, instead allow your mind to flow freely during the day and at night through your dreams. This is a potent week for the higher mind, which will enable you to truly plug yourself into it.

If you can manage to purify your life this week, then you will tune in to the powers that Pisces holds: insight, intuition and vision! Pisces "gone wrong" just wants to escape harsh realities or anything uncomfortable, and will try anything to drown out that truthful inner voice. Flush away fear and be brave, and by the end of the week you will be rewarded with some serious creative insights and solutions, delivered to you in ways you can actualize easily. The New Moon in Pisces is a powerful time to set out our intentions and, indeed, align with the spirit of the universe. Purify the mind and soul, then the heart will open and the rest will flow.

## Mission

- Review your daily habits and decide which are helpful and which restrict you.

- Decide to break a bad habit for at least one week and ask your circle to join you on your quest. Take it one day at a time.

- Make a pact to avoid alcohol, or anything else that is mind-altering, for this week at least.

- Keep a notebook or this journal with you to jot down insights and ideas.

- Unplug from daily noise and go to bed at the same time each night.

- Don't allow any electrical items to remain switched on while you sleep. Use candles to undress by, and remember to blow them out afterward!

*Aspiration/mantra:* **I am a channel for the higher mind.**

## Monday, February 17th

Mercury goes retrograde in Pisces. This is a good day on which to reflect and dream. It may not be charged with action, unless you have already set the wheels in motion before this retrograde.

**Mission completed?** Challenge level: 1–5: Ideas and insights:

## Tuesday, February 18th

The Moon moves into Capricorn, joining Mars, Jupiter and Pluto.
Mars and the Moon form an exact conjunction.
Power surge for Aquarius and Capricorn.

**Mission completed?** Challenge level: 1–5: Ideas and insights:

# Wednesday, February 19th

The Sun moves into Pisces.
Jupiter and the Moon are in perfect conjunction.

**Mission completed?** Challenge level: 1–5: Ideas and insights:

---

---

# Thursday, February 20th

Jupiter sextile Neptune.
The Moon is in Aquarius.
Power surge for Aquarius and Capricorn.

**Mission completed?** Challenge level: 1–5: Ideas and insights:

---

---

# Friday, February 21st

**Mission completed?** Challenge level: 1–5: Ideas and insights:

---

---

# Saturday, February 22nd

Power surge for Libra and Pisces.

**Mission completed?** Challenge level: 1–5: Ideas and insights:

---

---

## Sunday, February 23rd

The Moon moves into Pisces.

### New Moon in Pisces (10:32 AM EST)

● Write your New Moon intention list today; go back and forth creating it until you are sure you have everything down.

● Burn it safely and ask the universe to step in to manifest whatever is best for your soul and true path.

**Mission completed?** Challenge level: 1–5: Ideas and insights:

_____

_____

# Reflections ...

If you managed to complete this week's mission, how did it make you feel?

_____

_____

If you skipped anything, did you feel any different?

_____

_____

I did not include meditation in this week's mission. Did you notice a difference?

Did you feel the effects of Mercury retrograde this week?

Did you write a New Moon intention list?

Were there any light bulb moments or fresh ideas?

List a few things, or even just one, that you are grateful for.

Are there any takeaways from this week that you would like to address next week? Try reflecting without judgment.

# Monday, February 24th– Saturday, February 29th

## Forecast

This is a less complex week, with regards to the astrological energy. Aries seems to be running the show, beginning on Tuesday, so exercise and leading by example are musts, otherwise the energy may cause disruption. Exercise is not only vital to balance the mind, body and spirit, it also grounds the high-octane vibes that surround us right now.

If you have major stamps in Aries, then you're tasked this week with preventing any potential explosions. Steady the pace and channel the "gone right" traits of your opposite sign, Libra, which is skilled in diplomacy.

Try not to go over the top in your endeavors this week, or to exhaust yourself to the point of meltdown. Take it easy and maximize your energy by becoming mindful of what gives you energy and what, or who, drains it.

By Friday the mood mellows with the Moon's shift into the sign of Taurus; this has such a nourishing effect and asks that you slow down and appreciate all that you already have and already are.

## Mission

- Do your daily meditation practice each morning before you jump into your everyday life:
    - ○ Sit quietly and breathe slowly for ten minutes at least.
    - ○ Each time your mind wanders to the future, bring it back to the present with a deep breath.

- After your meditation, write a list of all that you would like to accomplish this week. It could be as simple as "Be kinder to myself" or as ambitious as "Close a deal." Whatever it is, try to consider a strategy to aid you. For example, if you wish to be happier in general, working on your mind with your daily meditation practice is a start, but then review what makes you happy and aim to find creative ways to do or have more of it.

*Aspiration/mantra*: **Be happy.**

## Monday, February 24th

**Mission completed?** Challenge level: 1–5: Ideas and insights:

_____

_____

## Tuesday, February 25th

The Moon moves into Aries.
Power surge for those with stamps in Aries and Capricorn.

**Mission completed?** Challenge level: 1–5: Ideas and insights:

_____

_____

## Wednesday, February 26th

The Moon connects to Venus in Aries. There should be plenty of upbeat energy to tap into today. It's a great time for presenting passionately and taking action; high-intensity workouts are also a good way to manage the double fire impact. Watch out for intolerance and exert patience.

**Mission completed?** Challenge level: 1–5: Ideas and insights:

---

## Thursday, February 27th

**Mission completed?** Challenge level: 1–5: Ideas and insights:

---

## Friday, February 28th

The Moon moves into Taurus.
Power surge for those with stamps in Capricorn and Taurus.

**Mission completed?** Challenge level: 1–5: Ideas and insights:

---

## Saturday, February 29th

**Mission completed?** Challenge level: 1–5: Ideas and insights:

---

# Reflections ...

If you managed to complete this week's mission, how did it make you feel?

If you skipped anything, did you feel any different?

Did you feel the effects of the daily meditation? If so, is this something that you will continue to do?

Did you write a list of all that you wanted to accomplish. How was that?

List a few things, or even just one, that you are grateful for.

Are there any takeaways from this week that you would like to address next week? Try reflecting without judgment.

Take a few moments to remember all the blessings this month, give yourself credit for the missions that you did achieve and relax before you skip into March.

_____

_____

_____

_____

# March

✺

W/e begin the month of March with the Sun in Pisces. March is commonly known as Pisces season and is the month most likely to allow us to do some astral-traveling and create some seriously profound art, while also finding inspiration for music, films and other creative pursuits.

Astrologically, this month is a perfect combination of water, fire and earth. We are attuned to listening to, and following, our dreams and chasing our desires. The first few weeks are prime for freeing up the imagination and working on big ideas and concepts, but not so hot for being on time, especially if we are on the nine-to-five conveyor belt.

"March" comes from the Roman name for Mars. Mars is the ruler of Aries and has always been known as the god of war, and so, historically, whenever March came around, it was considered the beginning of the season of conquering through warfare. It also marks the time when the mythological god of the underworld, Hades (a.k.a. Pluto, ruler of Scorpio), allowed his wife and queen, the goddess Persephone, to return to the Earth for one season (known as "spring") in order to appease her grief at being abducted into the darkness of the underworld.

## Signs in the Spotlight

*Pisces* (also its opposite sign, *Virgo*, to a lesser degree, until the Full Moon in Virgo on March 9th).

*Aquarius* (also its opposite sign, *Leo*, to a lesser degree).

*Taurus* (also its opposite sign, *Scorpio*, to a lesser degree).

*Aries* (also its opposite sign, *Libra*, to a lesser degree).

# The Return of the Light

March is celebrated in the northern hemisphere as the time when light returns, signaling the end of winter. We celebrate the Spring Equinox on March 20th, when the Sun crosses the equator, marking a new season. If you live in a land which experiences seasons, I am sure you are as relieved as Persephone to see green shoots begin to peep from the soil each spring.

Up until the 20th, when the Sun joins Aries, the weeks of March belong to Neptune, the ruler of Pisces and god of the seas and oceans. For this reason, it would be respectful to quit eating fish and anything else that is farmed to feed our voracious appetite for seafood. We cannot ignore the fact that the shift in consciousness is holding us more accountable than ever and we have to recognize the connection between ourselves, our great Divine Mother and all beings.

Spending time near the ocean will heal your soul this month and also give you a much deeper connection to the rhythms of the universe and life. If you have already quit eating fish, try to lead by example and open hearts and minds as to why. But remember not to judge, simply inspire! Support those who wish to wake up: show compassion, always use logic, and try not to switch to anger or allow emotions to obscure any opportunities for debate. March, or Mars, whichever you prefer, is historically known for waging wars. Make sure that your war is on ignorance and inertia, and let your weapons be facts. And let's win this!

# Beautiful Venus

Venus, the goddess of love, beauty and harmony, moves into Taurus on March 5th. Venus is the ruler of both Libra and Taurus, so this is a boost for both signs.

Taurus is more pragmatic than Pisces and Libra, generally speaking, and so this is a superb occasion to tune into the artistic flow of Pisces, along with the beautiful, talented and seriously pragmatic earth sign Taurus. We just have to watch out for being too worldly or materialistic under this influence, as this will push the visionary effect of Pisces far away and leave us with filters on photographs and no connection to soul. Taurus is all about nourishment and, while having the latest handbags or gadgets is surely satisfying to a degree, remember that sustainable is the new black, conscious is cool and ethical is sexy.

Love is also deeper than a mirror and your soul wishes to speak with you more than your smartphone does. Slow down and take care of yourself, and others, this month, both on a spiritual and physical level; your happiness will increase and simple pleasures will delight you.

# Mercury Is Direct in Aquarius

Mercury steps back into Aquarius now, and although it's still in a retrograde phase until March 10th, it's a marvelous time for tuning back in and raising our vibration in general, especially if we've lost our way in the last few weeks. Note that Aquarius allows genius to fuse with logic and this is not a time when selfish behavior will go unnoticed.

Mercury governs the individual and collective mind and the only downside to it joining Aquarius is the tendency to become fanatical. If you lose your temper, you've lost control. We need every warrior to be in top form, so balance your mind with meditation and your body with fresh air, exercise and sattvic (pure) food.

# Saturn Moves into Aquarius

Saturn has been in the sign of Capricorn since December 2017, and this is a huge shift. Saturn is important astrologically; it's a good idea to know where it is in your birth chart. If it has been, or is, connecting to any of your other planets, then it's a good idea to "master" whatever that planet represents.

It takes twenty-seven to twenty-eight years for Saturn to return to the place it was in when you were born, and that is what is known as your "Saturn Return." Saturn is the ancient ruler of Aquarius (as well as Uranus) and so is doubly powerful now for those of you born between January 1962 and March 1964, and February 1991 and May 1993, because it's your Saturn Return. Time to assess the lessons of the past and make moves to change that which no longer serves you.

Compassion is key here, as although Aquarius "gone right" combined with Saturn can be incredibly positive, it may cause some people to lack compassion and tolerance. It's a rebellious combination, and so we must crank up our "Aquarius gone right" traits to keep the balance.

Many people are fearful of Saturn connecting to their natal signs, as it causes us to remove the "rose-tinted" glasses and face reality. However, if we do not live in reality, reality comes to live with us! Saturn also prevents us from overindulging in areas of life that will not serve our karma well. Saturn is known as "Father Time" and, indeed, it is the planet of lessons, karma and past lives.

# International Women's Day

Maybe Madame Helena Blavatsky was right when she predicted that the Age of Aquarius would kick in in 1900 and all men and women would be seen as equals. In 1909, the Socialist Party of America organized the first ever National Women's Day as a focal point in the movement for women's rights. Revolutions spread fast, and only two years later International Women's Day was celebrated and over one million men and women campaigned for women's rights to work, vote, receive training and not suffer discrimination. It was only just over 100 years ago. How proud those people would be to see how far we have come. And we are so powerful when we are united as the brothers and sisters that we are.

*Pisces's mantra:* **I am a spiritual being living a physical existence.**

# Sunday, March 1st– Sunday, March 8th

## Forecast

Even for those of us who actively seek to live lives that balance our spiritual and worldly needs, it's easy to forget and lower our vibration to match the people we surround ourselves with. When we are spiritually aligned, we have the power to lift those people's vibrations too; when we are depleted, we just seem to sink. This is why it's so important to retreat from the humdrum and engage in regular spiritual practice and cleansing. This week is perfectly supported by the planets for exactly that. The draw to progress on a purely worldly level, no doubt due to the push from all the planets in Capricorn, will be around for many more months, but Pisces will not, so take as much time out as you can this week, and try not to numb the brain with television but instead listen to teachings. There are plenty of true spiritual teachers living simple lives and traveling in order to transmit deeper truths; you just need to look and you will find them.

Mercury's short move from Pisces into Aquarius will serve you well, no doubt eliminating all of the white noise and offering up suitable candidates for you to connect with and learn from, either through your own searches or via referrals from friends. Look out for them. One profound sentence from a wise and authentic being holds enough power to trigger a mind shift. Mercury is still retrograde this week, but this is a good time to revisit ideas that you may have left on the back burner, or anything that perhaps remains unresolved.

Venus shifts signs on Thursday, moving into the beautiful and earthy Taurus. Under this influence, it's not a week to push. Nurture your mind, be gentle with yourself and others, and plant seeds that you must patiently allow to grow at their own pace. Celebrate all of the women in your life, especially on the 8th, and say a quick thank you to all of the brave and wonderful men and women who have fought so hard for women's rights to be recognized and valued.

# Mission

Becoming aware of the presence of intuition is the first step to awakening it. So, practice this method each morning and keep an open mind:

- Every morning, for at least five minutes, sit quietly and gently focus on your breath. Enjoy the deep inhale; let tension go with the exhale.
- Take your first two fingers and gently rub your third eye, or pineal gland, also known as the third-eye chakra.
- Visualize flooding it with white light for a few breaths.
- Visualize it opening, helping you to gain clarity and increased intuition.
- Seek out a teacher and find their teachings online, or go to see them in person. Research them. Are they right for you? Trust your intuition!

*Aspiration/mantra:* **Align with your higher mind.**

## Sunday, March 1st

The Moon moves into Gemini.
Power surge for those with stamps in Capricorn and Gemini.

**Mission completed?** Challenge level: 1–5: Ideas and insights:

_____

_____

## Monday, March 2nd

**Mission completed?** Challenge level: 1–5: Ideas and insights:

_____

_____

## Tuesday, March 3rd

**Mission completed?** Challenge level: 1–5: Ideas and insights:

## Wednesday, March 4th

The Moon moves into Cancer.
Mercury retrogrades in Aquarius.
Power surge for those with stamps in Cancer, Libra and Taurus.

**Mission completed?** Challenge level: 1–5: Ideas and insights:

## Thursday, March 5th

Venus moves into Taurus.

**Mission completed?** Challenge level: 1–5: Ideas and insights:

## Friday, March 6th

The Moon moves into Leo. This is a wonderful day to embrace passion projects and to spend time on anything, or with anyone, that helps expand your heart. Power surge for those with major stamps in Capricorn and Leo.

**Mission completed?** Challenge level: 1–5: Ideas and insights:

## Saturday, March 7th

**Mission completed?** Challenge level: 1–5: Ideas and insights:

_____

_____

## Sunday, March 8th

**Happy International Women's Day!**
Remind the women in your life just how much they have positively impacted you!
Send a silent thank you to all people who campaigned for equal rights. We owe
them such gratitude for the rights and opportunities we often take for granted.

The Moon moves into Virgo. Avoid any negative words today; keep the energy
high with loving kindness to yourself and others. It's a good day to focus on
any tasks that you may have been avoiding, as this will increase your sense of
satisfaction and decrease anxiety.
Power surge for those with stamps in Aquarius, Gemini and Virgo.

**Mission completed?** Challenge level: 1–5: Ideas and insights:

_____

_____

# Reflections ...

If you managed to complete this week's mission, how did it make you feel?

_____

_____

If you skipped anything, did you feel any different?

_____

_____

Did you notice feeling different when Venus moved from Aries to Taurus?

_____

_____

Did you remember, and honor, the special women who have inspired you on International Women's Day?

_____

_____

How did the week's aspiration unfold? Did it help you tune in to your higher mind?

_____

_____

List a few things, or even just one, that you are grateful for.

_____

_____

Are there any takeaways from this week that you would like to address next week? Try reflecting without judgment.

_____

_____

# Monday, March 9th– Sunday, March 15th

## Forecast

This week begins with a Full Moon in Virgo, so writing down all that you wish to release will free you up for the rest of the month.

Virgo is a sign that is happiest when it feels in control, yet we all know that the universe is actually in control, and when we surrender to the fact that we can only do so much, this will push us to focus on what's most important and then let go of the rest, which is key in a Full Moon phase. This Full Moon is in Virgo, and when this sign goes wrong, it makes us more prone to be doubtful and even negative, so using your breathing techniques, along with some simple meditation, will help soothe your mind this week.

Admitting and embracing your vulnerabilities will also allow unseen forces to come to your rescue and assist you in ways that you may never have imagined.

Mercury goes direct in Aquarius this week, so the mission for the week ahead will boost your ability to be creative and feel liberated!

## Mission

In order to honor the Full Moon in Virgo you need to channel the "gone right" traits of this sign: order, organization and purity. This will help you to navigate negativity and feelings of doubt, using the Mercury shift to assist your worldly and spiritual progress.

- Meditate every morning for at least ten minutes.

- Clear your space one room at a time. Be ruthless with anything you do not need – give it to charity or recycle it. Try the following:

  ○ Declutter and organize a room.

  ○ Buy some frankincense resin, a small piece of coal and an unbreakable dish.

  ○ Use a vacuum cleaner to go around the corners of the ordered room, asking for negative, stagnant energy to be removed.

  ○ Light the small piece of coal, place the resin on top and open the windows, then ask all negative and stagnant energy to leave. Let the room "settle."

  ○ If you and your family notice the difference (and you will!), repeat the process slowly and thoroughly.

*Aspiration/mantra*: **Clear your space!**

# Monday, March 9th

## Full Moon in Virgo (1:48 PM EDT)

- Write a list of worries and issues that you would like to remove from your life, then burn it and ask the universe to remove them all.

Also know that life isn't perfect. The best spiritual teachers would all testify that suffering enables us to progress, for although certain situations are seemingly beyond our control, we always have the power to handle situations with grace. In the East they believe karma is magnified under the Full and New Moon phases, so work on sidestepping anything negative and watch your words and thoughts in order to remain positive and productive.

**Mission completed?** Challenge level: 1–5: Ideas and insights:

_____

_____

## Tuesday, March 10th

The Moon moves into Libra.
Mercury goes direct in Aquarius.
It's a marvelous day to make peace and harmonize our professional and personal relationships.
Power surge for those with major stamps in Capricorn and Libra.

**Mission completed?** Challenge level: 1–5: Ideas and insights:

_____

_____

## Wednesday, March 11th

**Mission completed?** Challenge level: 1–5: Ideas and insights:

_____

_____

## Thursday, March 12th

The Moon moves into Scorpio.
Power surge for those with stamps in Capricorn and Scorpio.

**Mission completed?** Challenge level: 1–5: Ideas and insights:

_____

_____

## Friday, March 13th

The origin of the superstition of Friday the 13th bringing bad luck is hard to confirm. Some believe it's because Judas, who betrayed Jesus, was the thirteenth apostle, and some historians say that the origins of Friday the 13th being unlucky dates back to 1907, when a book was published declaring that both Fridays and the number thirteen were unlucky, and the superstition seeded out from there … However, as we know, we make our own luck!

**Mission completed?** Challenge level: 1–5: Ideas and insights:

## Saturday, March 14th

The Moon moves into Sagittarius. Time to unplug from the digital world and get outside in order to seek out nature, and rejuvenate naturally.
Power surge for those with major stamps in Capricorn and Sagittarius.

**Mission completed?** Challenge level: 1–5: Ideas and insights:

## Sunday, March 15th

**Mission completed?** Challenge level: 1–5: Ideas and insights:

# Reflections ...

If you managed to complete this week's mission, how did it make you feel?

_____

_____

If you skipped anything, did you feel any different?

_____

_____

Did you complete the Full Moon ritual? How did it make you feel?

_____

_____

How did the week's aspiration unfold?

_____

_____

List a few things, or even just one, that you are grateful for.

_____

_____

Are there any takeaways from this week that you would like to address next week? Try reflecting without judgment.

_____

_____

# Monday, March 16th– Sunday, March 22nd

## Forecast

This week begins with the Moon in Capricorn, which is fabulous for achievement and hard work leading to tangible results. If Capricorn is your Moon sign, you should feel emotionally strong! Of course, it's also powerful for those with the Sun and other major stamps in Capricorn, and in Cancer, its opposite sign.

Saturn, the master of karma and life lessons, shifts from Capricorn into Aquarius this week, and this is huge. Saturn hasn't hit this sign since February 1991, and it signifies a time of mass awakening and revolution. It is particularly significant for anyone with Saturn, the Sun and other major stamps in Aquarius, but it asks us all to review our lives and take humanity as a whole into consideration. No pressure!

Whatever your birth chart, take it easy this week and avoid feeling pressured; prepare for a few reviews and trust in the process of change. It's better not to resist change; it's more effective to listen to the quiet voice in your heart, which will lead you in the right direction. Moderation is key this week.

## Mission

Meditation is also key this week, especially for those of you entering your Saturn Return. You need to allow yourself the space and freedom to listen to your higher mind and attune to universal wisdom.

- This week could push you to review your belief systems and experience some mind-blowing deeper truths and revelations. Any time you feel overwhelmed, take three deep breaths and release the tension before you react or respond to anything or anyone.

- Make lists of all that you hope to achieve.
- Make lists of all that you have already achieved.
- Relax.

*Aspiration/mantra:* **I am open to positive change.**

## Monday, March 16th

The Moon moves into Capricorn.
Mercury moves into Pisces.
Power surge for those with major stamps in Capricorn and Pisces.

**Mission completed?** Challenge level: 1–5: Ideas and insights:

## Tuesday, March 17th

**Mission completed?** Challenge level: 1–5: Ideas and insights:

## Wednesday, March 18th

**Mission completed?** Challenge level: 1–5: Ideas and insights:

## Thursday, March 19th

The Moon moves into Aquarius.
Power surge for those with stamps in Aquarius, Capricorn and Cancer.

**Mission completed?** Challenge level: 1–5: Ideas and insights:

---

## Friday, March 20th

The Sun moves into Aries.
Power surge for Aries, Aquarius, Libra, Pisces and Taurus.
The equinox is when the Sun is exactly above the equator and the hours of daytime and nighttime are roughly equal. In the northern hemisphere, today is the Spring (Vernal) Equinox; in the southern hemisphere, it signals the end of summer and beginning of autumn (or fall), so it's the Autumnal Equinox. For northern hemisphere folks, it's a great time for a party to welcome the return of Persephone!

**Mission completed?** Challenge level: 1–5: Ideas and insights:

---

## Saturday, March 21st

The Moon moves into Pisces.

**Mission completed?** Challenge level: 1–5: Ideas and insights:

## Sunday, March 22rd

Saturn moves into Aquarius.
Power surge for Aquarius.

**Mission completed?** Challenge level: 1–5: Ideas and insights:

_____

_____

# Reflections ...

If you managed to complete this week's mission, how did it make you feel?

_____

_____

If you skipped anything, did you feel any different?

_____

_____

Did you notice feeling any different when Saturn changed signs?

_____

_____

How did the week's aspiration unfold?

_____

_____

List a few things, or even just one, that you are grateful for.

_____

_____

Are there any takeaways from this week that you would like to address next week? Try reflecting without judgment.

_____

_____

# Monday, March 23rd– Sunday, March 29th

## Forecast

There is a New Moon in Aries on Tuesday, which is an almighty boost for any of us who have been lacking in motivation or energy. By the time the weekend hits, we will be enjoying the beautiful and wholesome vibes sent via Venus and the Moon in Taurus. This weekend is an important time to recoup our energy and heal from life in the fast lane, including the random electrifying flashes sent by Saturn in Aquarius, which can push us even when we have nothing left to give. Make sure you unplug and take time out in nature.

## Mission

Meditate every morning for at least ten minutes, even if your ego resists. Partake in some gentle stretching, twisting and relaxation exercises:

- Stand up, close your eyes and take a few deep breaths.
- Inhale; sweep your arms above your head, palms together, lengthen the spine and look at your thumbs. Exhale slowly, bringing your hands back to the side of your body.
- Repeat several times until you feel energized and relaxed.

*Aspiration/mantra:* **I nourish my mind, body and soul.**

## Monday, March 23rd

Power surge for those with major stamps in Aries and Capricorn.

**Mission completed?** Challenge level: 1–5: Ideas and insights:

_____

_____

## Tuesday, March 24th

### New Moon in Aries (5:28 AM EDT)

- Write a New Moon intention list. Include all that you are grateful for and add in all the things that you would like, as if you already have them. This is a powerfully karmic time, so be sure to add in something altruistic.

- Contemplate all that you wish to manifest and burn the list.

PS Don't add anything that will bring someone else sorrow, this is not going to earn you any good karma cookies. Have faith in your power and path!

**Mission completed?** Challenge level: 1–5: Ideas and insights:

_____

_____

## Wednesday, March 25th

**Mission completed?** Challenge level: 1–5: Ideas and insights:

_____

_____

## Thursday, March 26th

The Moon moves into Taurus.
Power surge for those with major stamps in Aries, Capricorn and Taurus.

**Mission completed?** Challenge level: 1–5: Ideas and insights:

---

## Friday, March 27th

**Mission completed?** Challenge level: 1–5: Ideas and insights:

---

## Saturday, March 28th

Exact conjunction between Venus and Moon in Taurus.
Today is wonderful for cultivating deep contentment, so spend time with loved ones in a beautiful setting that is as natural as possible.
Power surge for those with stamps in Aries, Capricorn and Gemini.

**Mission completed?** Challenge level: 1–5: Ideas and insights:

---

## Sunday, March 29th

The Moon moves into Gemini.
Power surge for those with stamps in Aries, Capricorn, Sagittarius and Gemini.

**Mission completed?** Challenge level: 1–5: Ideas and insights:

---

# Reflections ...

If you managed to complete this week's mission, how did it make you feel?

_____

_____

If you skipped anything, did you feel any different?

_____

_____

Did you notice feeling different under the New Moon in Aries? Did you write your list?

_____

_____

How did the week's aspiration unfold?

_____

_____

List a few things, or even just one, that you are grateful for.

_____

_____

Are there any takeaways from this week that you would like to address next week? Try reflecting without judgment.

_____

_____

# Monday, March 30th– Tuesday, March 31st

## Forecast

The rest of this month is dominated by Aquarius and fellow air sign, Gemini, and so it's likely to be a busy end to the month.

This is a smart time to think, strategize and put together cunning plans that will achieve the most and serve humanity.

Due to Saturn's shift last week there is much emphasis on how we "serve" the wider community and what we are doing to help not only humanity but also the planet.

Mars governs our energy and it moves into the sign of Aquarius on Monday, until May, so compassion will be evoked for ourselves and others. Aquarius is also the sign that triggers ingenuity, which is marvelous, but remember the fine line between genius and insanity: walk the line like a ballerina while protecting your mind with spiritual practice and your body with some powerful enhanced exercise.

## Mission

- Meditate every morning for at least ten minutes.
- Volunteer for a charity in some way, and donate skills or resources, rather than money, though this is fine too!
- On both days, give some food or drink to a homeless person, without telling anyone.

*Aspiration/mantra:* **I am part of the solution.**

## Monday, March 30th

Mars moves into Aquarius.
Power surge for those with stamps in Aquarius, Cancer and Pisces.

**Mission completed?** Challenge level: 1–5: Ideas and insights:

_____

_____

## Tuesday, March 31st

**Mission completed?** Challenge level: 1–5: Ideas and insights:

_____

_____

# Reflections ...

If you managed to complete the mission, how did it make you feel?

_____

_____

If you skipped anything, did you feel any different?

_____

_____

How did the last two days' aspiration unfold?

_____

_____

List a few things, or even just one, that you are grateful for.

Are there any takeaways from this week that you would like to address next week? Try reflecting without judgment.

Next month is almost here, so appreciate all you have achieved and relax before you move on to April.

# April

pril is derived from the Latin word *Aprillis*, which means "to open." In the northern hemisphere, it's usually the time when the buds begin to open and the world blooms. "April" also stems from the goddess Aphrodite, otherwise known as Venus, ruler of Taurus and Libra. The Sun is in Aries until April 19th, when it moves into Taurus. Aries and strong stamps in Taurus is a supreme combination in a personal chart; Aries is a known pioneer and Taurus is multi-skilled and talented, and neither sign is content until they make stuff happen and bring ideas to life. Think Leonardo da Vinci, Vincent Van Gogh and those who used the written word to raise awareness and spark change. Charlotte Brontë was born in April and she used storytelling to bring strong-minded powerful females to prominence in an era when women had few rights. William Wordsworth and Maya Angelou are also among the artistic and literary avant-garde who were born this month.

## Signs in the Spotlight

 *Aries* (also its opposite sign, *Libra*, to a lesser degree, until the Full Moon in Libra on April 8th).

 *Taurus* (also its opposite sign, *Scorpio*, to a lesser degree).

 *Aquarius* (also its opposite sign, *Leo*, to a lesser degree).

 *Capricorn* (also its opposite sign, *Cancer*, to a lesser degree).

# Fresh Starts and New Beginnings

This month is ripe for courage, fresh starts and beginnings for those who wish to launch new businesses and start-ups; the energy is there to give birth to something incredible. Aries is a fire sign and while the ram isn't usually known for patience, it's a dynamic, powerful and effective sign, and one usually comfortable with risk. Great leaders are more often than not born with plenty of Aries in their chart, as they rarely fail to take the initiative and forge ahead to implement change and achieve success. Aries folks can also be extremely competitive, which can be annoying, but they do make fabulous athletes.

# Rebirth and Resurrection

April is brimming with celebrations. Wherever you live and whatever your culture, rebirth and freedom from oppression are instilled in your psyche on some level this month. We observe Arab American Heritage Month, which recognizes the contributions of the Arab Americans to humanity, and the Christian festival of Easter and the Jewish Passover are also celebrated this month.

The tradition of giving Easter eggs is said to come from the tomb of Jesus after his crucifixion, which was empty but actually indicated his resurrection and indeed a "new life" or reincarnation. The "Easter bunny" tradition simply comes from rabbits, who give birth to many babies in spring, illustrating new life. The actual date of Easter Sunday is chosen in accordance with the Full Moon. It is the first Sunday after the first Full Moon after the Spring Equinox.

# Spiritual Beings

Irrespective of our birth heritage, we are all connected as spiritual beings; our spirits have no color or nationality.

What we do with our lives here on Earth is down to us; we have the power to elevate our souls and progress no matter what hand life has dealt us. Spring is the time when we leave behind the shackles of the past and embrace what time we have to live in harmony with one another and prosper, the point being that we have more in common than not. True progress is reflected in our ability to understand one another based purely on our character and our deeds, not on our beliefs or backgrounds.

# Spring-Clean for your Soul

In Finland, April is called *huhtikuu,* which means "slash and burn moon," and April is their time for clearing farmland and felling dead wood. We need to create fresh energy in our life and in order to do that, we are urged to clear away the debris and dead wood. And so, taking inspiration from the Finns, clear your space. If any aspect of your life is cluttered, even if it's in the digital "cloud," on a deeper level it restricts the flow of positive energy toward you. The most successful creatives I know are organized and minimalistic, and as far as I am concerned, creativity is our soul speaking. Every person on Earth has creativity in their soul, it's just often tightly wrapped in the humdrum of worldly life and can't find a way out. But we can all be creative – it isn't reserved for the artistically talented. Cooking is creative; gardening is creative, and finding simple solutions for complex issues is the best ingenuity of them all.

# Transformation and Opportunity

Jupiter and Pluto in Capricorn form an exact conjunction on April 5th, and this is an almighty partnership: opportunities influenced by Jupiter's expansive output are fused with Pluto's supremacy. Transformation is inevitable if we are to embrace the "gone right" potentials for this combination. We need to face ourselves honestly, and ruthlessly tackle the areas of life that forge our commitments. Breakthroughs in the professional environment are likely and sometimes leaving a career behind is simply written in the stars. Pluto unceremoniously pulls the rug if we ignore the subtle messages from the universe, imploring us to change our ways and take the bigger picture into consideration. It's deep.

# Relationships and Connections

By the time the Full Moon in Libra graces our planet on April 8th, it's tactical to review our relationships. Which serve us and which lower our vibration and standards in general? The people in our life impact us the most, and it's time to be honest about who in our close circles inspires and encourages the best versions of ourselves and who does the opposite. Don't be afraid to step away from people who lower your standards, for as one door closes, others soon open. Never burn any bridges – that is not what we are here for – just execute grace and quietly step away until your example leads others, directly or indirectly.

Venus moves into Gemini on April 3rd, inspiring our heart and filling us with the impetus to seek stimulation and excitement.

*Aries's mantra:* **I am reborn and I lead by my own example.**

# Wednesday, April 1st–
# Sunday, April 5th

## Forecast

This week is brimming with inspiration and opportunity, and it's worth noting that opportunity isn't always directly related to worldly achievements or money. Anything that triggers our heart and activates our mind is the best form of opportunity, as this serves our soul.

On Tuesday and Wednesday there is a standoff between Aquarius and Leo, and we are pushed to review what is selfish or solely self-serving in our life. If you encounter these ugly traits in others, have compassion and perhaps use this alignment to educate them with love or leave them behind. We have all been directed toward a selfish vision for long enough, and this will not help any of us in the long run. The sooner we all realize that we are connected to every rhythm and heartbeat on the planet, the faster we shall progress. If you are stuck in a false reality, believing that the narcissistic people in your life and in the public eye are living their best lives, wake up to the fact (if you haven't already) that the eye of karma never misses a beat, and if people do nothing but serve themselves, they run the risk of depleting all the positive karma they have generated in past lives. We have to balance the books and look beyond one life, which is nothing more than a flash. Karma is certainly not $a + b = c$; it is a universal law that cannot be manipulated.

## Mission

- Meditate for at least ten minutes each day.

- Give yourself one additional task each day. This could be as simple as "Say good morning to a stranger" or "Go for a walk" or as complex as "Clear all my paperwork." But whatever you choose, make it achievable, or you run the risk of missing the whole point!

*Aspiration/mantra:* **I attract real people.**

# Wednesday, April 1st

**April Fool's Day.**
Before we switched from the Julian calendar to the Gregorian, April 1st was celebrated as New Year and those who forgot the change were playfully called "April fools."

The Moon is in Cancer. You may be prone to take things personally, so keep a healthy perspective.

**Mission completed?** Challenge level: 1–5: Ideas and insights:

---

# Thursday, April 2nd

The Moon moves into Leo. Saturn in Aquarius and Mars in Aquarius form an opposition to the Moon in Leo.
Power surge for those with major stamps in Aquarius, Taurus, Libra and Leo.

**Mission completed?** Challenge level: 1–5: Ideas and insights:

---

# Friday, April 3rd

Venus moves into Gemini. For the next few days, it's likely that you will be busy and experience an increase in tasks, emails, phone calls and communications in general. Try to stay grounded and focused.
Power surge for those with major stamps in Aries and Virgo.

**Mission completed?** Challenge level: 1–5: Ideas and insights:

---

## Saturday, April 4th

The Moon moves into Virgo. This weekend is perfect to carry out a "spring-cleaning." Do so in any way you can.

**Mission completed?** Challenge level: 1–5: Ideas and insights:

---

## Sunday, April 5th

Jupiter conjoins Pluto in Capricorn. At this time it's more effective to focus on your achievements than on all you have not yet managed. Give yourself a break and be optimistic and pragmatic.

**Mission completed?** Challenge level: 1–5: Ideas and insights:

---

# Reflections ...

If you managed to complete this week's mission, how did it make you feel?

---

If you skipped anything, did you feel any different?

_____

_____

Did you notice any overtly selfish behavior around you and, if so, how did you handle it?

_____

_____

How did the week's aspiration unfold? Did it help you notice the real people you encountered?

_____

_____

List a few things, or even just one, that you are grateful for.

_____

_____

Are there any takeaways from this week that you would like to address next week? Try reflecting without judgment.

_____

_____

# Monday, April 6th– Sunday, April 12th

## Forecast

This week is all about Libra and the impact of the sign's energy output may push us to review our relationships and unions in general. We will no doubt be offered many opportune moments this week to become more peaceful and diplomatic.

This week also encourages us to address any aspects of our life that are unbalanced. Blaming other people for the way they treat or mistreat us is counterproductive and we would be wise to advocate changes that redress the balance without aggression or anger. The whole Libran vibe is prevalent on Monday and Tuesday, with the Full Moon in Libra on Wednesday as the finale. This beautiful Full Moon is when we release all the expectations that were never met by certain people and situations. Expectation and comparison are the fastest routes to disappointment, and the only expectations we need to focus on are our own. The rest is acceptance of what actually is, which leads to peace! So, let it go …

## Mission

- Meditate every morning to restore your balance and cultivate inner harmony:
  - Sit in silence in the same place every morning, close your laptop and switch off your phone.
  - Sit quietly for ten minutes (more if you can) and take deep purposeful breaths in through your nose and out through your mouth. Hold the intention of peace in your heart and mind.

○ Don't argue with anyone or allow an angry word to spill from your lips this week. If you slip up, apologize immediately (even to yourself), no matter who is "right."

*Aspiration/mantra:* **I am peaceful.**

## Monday, April 6th

The Moon moves into Libra.
Power surge for those with major stamps in Capricorn and Libra.

**Mission completed?** Challenge level: 1–5: Ideas and insights:

_____

_____

## Tuesday, April 7th

**Mission completed?** Challenge level: 1–5: Ideas and insights:

_____

_____

## Wednesday, April 8th

**Passover starts.**

## Full Moon in Libra (4:25 PM EDT)

The Moon moves into the empowering sign of Scorpio at 4:25 PM EDT.

Power surge for those with major stamps in Aries, Libra, Capricorn, Taurus and Scorpio.

- Light some candles and burn some natural incense. You may do this alone or engage your partner and family to take part and release anything they wish to let go of.

- Write down all the aspects of your life that are unbalanced. Forget solutions – those will follow later – this ritual is all about release.

- Burn your list and thank the Moon Goddess for removing the obstacles and imbalance.

**Mission completed?** Challenge level: 1–5: Ideas and insights:

# Thursday, April 9th

**Mission completed?** Challenge level: 1–5: Ideas and insights:

# Friday, April 10th

The Moon moves into Sagittarius.
Power surge for those with major stamps in Pisces, Gemini and Sagittarius.

**Mission completed?** Challenge level: 1–5: Ideas and insights:

_____

_____

# Saturday, April 11th

Mercury moves into Aries. This evokes action and sparks of inspiration and dynamism, but be mindful not to lose patience with yourself or others.

**Mission completed?** Challenge level: 1–5: Ideas and insights:

_____

_____

# Sunday, April 12th

**Easter Sunday.**
Power surge for those with major stamps in Gemini, Leo and Capricorn.

**Mission completed?** Challenge level: 1–5: Ideas and insights:

_____

_____

# Reflections ...

If you managed to complete this week's mission, how did it make you feel?

If you skipped anything, did you feel any different?

How was your Full Moon ritual?

Did you become aware of any imbalance in your life?

List a few things, or even just one, that you are grateful for.

Are there any takeaways from this week that you would like to address next week? Try reflecting without judgment.

# Monday, April 13th– Saturday, April 19th

## Forecast

This week is overflowing with higher vibrational frequencies and a feeling of unity and compassion. On Wednesday there is an advanced connection between Saturn, Mars and the Moon in Aquarius; this is a brilliant time to evoke compassion and tolerance for yourself and others. It also opens us up, enabling us to notice the changing rhythms of the universe. Mars activates higher wisdom and the Moon ensures we actually begin to feel connected.

This makes it an ideal week to study any subject that has the potential to expand your mind. Remember, though, that while this is the star potential, the reality is down to you and the choices you make. Seek out wisdom and be open to receiving random information that is both simple and profound.

Friendships are well starred this week, and forging new ones or strengthening existing bonds could be a focus.

## Mission

- Meditate every morning and try to do the same each night for a minimum of ten minutes. This week could deliver updates to the programming of your mind! So, being open and clearing the channels would serve you well.

- In addition to this, as is always the way with a major Aquarian-led alignment, the potential to short-circuit or get wires crossed is high, so unplug and if you have a partner or family, ask them to support you in your quest.

- The Sun moves into Taurus on Sunday, so it will be wonderful to spend time with loved ones and focus on the simple pleasures. Unplug! Buy books and read a new chapter each night. My suggestions: *The Prophet*, Kahlil Gibran; *The Monk Who Sold His Ferrari*, Robin Sharma; *The Dance of 17 Lives*, Mick Brown; *1984*, George Orwell.

*Aspiration/mantra:* **I align with high-vibrational frequencies.**

## Monday, April 13th

The Moon moves into Capricorn.

**Mission completed?** Challenge level: 1–5: Ideas and insights:

---

## Tuesday, April 14th

Power surge for those with major stamps in Capricorn, Sagittarius and Aquarius.

**Mission completed?** Challenge level: 1–5: Ideas and insights:

---

## Wednesday, April 15th

The Moon moves into Aquarius.
Exact conjunction between Saturn, Mars and the Moon in Aquarius.

**Mission completed?** Challenge level: 1–5: Ideas and insights:

---

# Thursday, April 16th

**Passover ends.**

**Mission completed?** Challenge level: 1–5: Ideas and insights:

# Friday, April 17th

The Moon moves into Pisces.
Power surge for those with major stamps in Aries, Leo and Pisces.

**Mission completed?** Challenge level: 1–5: Ideas and insights:

# Saturday, April 18th

**Mission completed?** Challenge level: 1–5: Ideas and insights:

# Sunday, April 19th

The Sun moves into Taurus.
Power surge for those with major stamps in Taurus, Scorpio, Capricorn, Sagittarius and Aries.

**Mission completed?** Challenge level: 1–5: Ideas and insights:

# Reflections ...

If you managed to complete this week's mission, how did it make you feel?

_____

_____

If you skipped anything, did you feel any different?

_____

_____

Did you find a good book and read?

_____

_____

After unplugging at night did you feel a difference in the morning?

_____

_____

List a few things, or even just one, that you are grateful for.

_____

_____

Are there any takeaways from this week that you would like to address next week? Try reflecting without judgment.

_____

_____

# Monday, 20th April– Sunday, 26th April

## Forecast

The Sun is now in Taurus and so taking into account the ways in which we nourish ourselves is more important than ever. The food we eat is literally our fuel and if we are not already aware of the impact toxic food and drinks have on us, this is the week to test it out. Every time we eat an animal, we should be mindful that we are also taking in all that it has consumed in its lifetime, including through industrial farming practices, and unless you raise your own livestock, you cannot guarantee that the animal has had a healthy and happy life. If you are vegetarian, quit all animal products for the week's mission. If you are vegan, recommend vegan recipes and restaurants or cook delicious vegan food for everyone else.

## Mission

The Moon in Aries provides us with impeccable timing to start something new. At least try the mission this week and evaluate how you actually feel, how your mind is and how much energy you have. Taurus is only ever interested in tangible results, and if something provides real benefits, they will stick with it.

This week the main focus is total mind, body and spirit alignment, so we will embrace a mission that serves all three:

- Begin each day with at least ten minutes of meditation and gentle breathing:
  - Sit up straight and close your eyes, breathe deeply in through your nose and out through your nose.
  - Focus on returning to the breath when your mind jumps around (and it will!).

- Try to quit eating anything that had a pulse; plan your meals in advance if you need to, and research delicious and nutritious new recipes to create.

- Exercise for at least fifteen minutes each day. It could be walking, running, Yoga or whatever you like, but try not to set yourself up for failure by committing to too much if you're not used to it.

*Aspiration/mantra:* **My body is a temple; my mind is a shrine.**

# Monday, April 20th

The Moon moves into Aries.

**Mission completed?** Challenge level: 1–5: Ideas and insights:

---

---

# Tuesday, April 21st

**Mission completed?** Challenge level: 1–5: Ideas and insights:

---

---

## Wednesday, April 22nd

### New Moon in Taurus (9:36 PM EDT)

This is the perfect time to adopt new ways of living that enhance your overall well-being and nourish you. Think of sustainability!

- Recruit some of your friends and family to join you, as the power of the ritual is magnified when a few people unite and all have positive intentions.

- Light some candles and natural incense. Write your intention list.

- Contemplate all the requests, burn the list and thank the Moon Goddess for providing you with all you need to sustain a long, healthy and happy life.

The Moon moves into Taurus.
Power surge for those with major stamps in Capricorn, Sagittarius and Taurus.

**Mission completed?** Challenge level: 1–5: Ideas and insights:

## Thursday, April 23rd

**Mission completed?** Challenge level: 1–5: Ideas and insights:

## Friday, April 24th

**Mission completed?** Challenge level: 1–5: Ideas and insights:

_____

_____

## Saturday, April 25th

The Moon moves into Gemini.
Pluto goes retrograde in Capricorn.
Power surge for those with major stamps in Capricorn, Gemini and Sagittarius.

**Mission completed?** Challenge level: 1–5: Ideas and insights:

_____

_____

## Sunday, April 26th

**Mission completed?** Challenge level: 1–5: Ideas and insights:

_____

_____

# Reflections ...

If you managed to complete this week's mission, how did it make you feel?

_____

_____

If you skipped anything, did you feel any different?

Did you manage to quit eating animals or animal products? How did you find it? How challenging was it, and how did it make you feel?

Did you take part in a New Moon ritual?

How did the week's aspiration unfold? Did it help you to be kinder to your mind, body and spirit?

List a few things, or even just one, that you are grateful for.

Are there any takeaways from this week that you would like to address next week? Try reflecting without judgment.

# Monday, April 27th– Thursday, April 30th

## Forecast

Mercury moves into Taurus and joins the Sun, which is such a splendid combination, it has potential to infuse us with beneficial healing and uplifting energy. We may be more sensitive than usual on Tuesday, as the Moon in Cancer's energy is magnified by Jupiter in the opposite sign of Capricorn. Try not to be too harsh on yourself and really focus on the talent Taurus has to just "be." Be in the moment; be yourself. Appreciation will attract more of the same, and this week should bring real fruits from all your recent endeavors. By the time the Moon moves into Leo on Thursday, you will likely be ready for some fun and anything that makes you feel sunny and happy. Take some time out to appreciate all that you already are! And be happy – that serves the universe in bigger ways than you can comprehend. Be in the moment, too, be present in all that you do and be true to yourself!

## Mission

Meditation helps to train your mind to stay in the moment; living in the past is not healthy and can lead to sadness, while jumping into the future can cause anxiety, so the only real peace is to be found in the present moment. Taurus especially can suffer with their shoulders and backs, so the following exercises will enable you to loosen up and not become too "fixed":

- Meditate for at least ten minutes first thing in the morning without checking your phone (unless it's to see the time or set an alarm). If you do check your phone, it will drag you into the past or the future.

- Repeat the following exercises extremely slowly, several times each, or at least until you feel any tension leave you:

- ○ Stand up straight. Slouch forward, then, on the inhale, roll your shoulders back.

- ○ Repeat the exercise, exhaling as you slouch forward.

- ○ Now gently let your head roll forward, giving you a double chin effect! Inhale gently, lift your head back and exhale as you roll it gently forward again.

- ○ Inhale, then move your shoulder blades up and back with the aim of trying to make them meet. You won't, unless of course you are a contortionist, but that is simply to give you the idea!

*Aspiration/mantra:* **Just be.**

## Monday, April 27th

The Moon moves into Cancer.
Mercury moves into Taurus.
Power surge for those with major stamps in Aries, Cancer and Gemini.

**Mission completed?** Challenge level: 1–5: Ideas and insights:

## Tuesday, April 28th

**Mission completed?** Challenge level: 1–5: Ideas and insights:

## Wednesday, April 29th

Power surge for those with major stamps in Sagittarius, Capricorn and Leo.

**Mission completed?** Challenge level: 1–5: Ideas and insights:

_____

_____

## Thursday, April 30th

The Moon moves into Leo.

**Mission completed?** Challenge level: 1–5: Ideas and insights:

_____

_____

# Reflections ...

If you managed to complete this week's mission, how did it make you feel?

_____

_____

If you skipped anything, did you feel any different?

_____

_____

Did you feel a release of tension with the exercises?

Did you feel a mental shift when Mercury shifted into Taurus?

How did the week's aspiration unfold? Did it increase your ability to stay present?

List a few things, or even just one, that you are grateful for.

Are there any takeaways from this week that you would like to address next week? Try reflecting without judgment.

Take a few moments to reflect on this month and just let yourself be before you move on to May.

# May

☼

M ay was named after Maia, the Greek goddess of fertility, and in many countries in the northern hemisphere the official start of spring is celebrated now. It's also known as Taurus season. Taurus, as a sign and time, is directly linked with beauty. The flowers that grace us this month are more than just pretty faces; they are purifying in many ways, as we will see below. Taurus season is one where we are asked to examine our resources and celebrate the Great Mother to whom we all belong.

## Signs in the Spotlight

 *Taurus* (also its opposite sign, *Scorpio*, to a lesser degree, until the Full Moon in Scorpio on May 7th).

 *Gemini* (also its opposite sign, *Sagittarius*, to a lesser degree).

 *Aquarius* (also its opposite sign, *Leo*, to a lesser degree).

 *Pisces* (also its opposite sign, *Virgo*, to a lesser degree).

# Feng Shui for Everyone

The practice of feng shui, which has been around for thousands of years, can be used to increase positive energy and the flow of abundance. Certain plants and flowers, particularly bamboo, are believed to attract well-being and wealth, deflect negative energies and offer protection from negative forces. In simple terms, flowers and plants have the power to transform negativity; in Holland in the seventeenth century, tulips were actually classified as more valuable than gold and were used as currency.

May belongs to the sign of Taurus until the 20th, when the Sun moves on to influence Gemini. As a personal sign or collective energy, Taurus is absolutely beautiful, and it is as tenacious as it is unyielding, which can go right or wrong depending on the particular focus of the person channeling it. May is the only month that always starts and ends on the same day of the week, which is pretty typical of the earth sign Taurus, which distrusts change, preferring tradition and consistency over the spontaneity and randomness enjoyed by most fire and air signs.

# Natural Grace and Beauty

May and Taurus are both associated with natural beauty and grace, and this energy is as resourceful as nature itself. Just as trees blossom and flowers bloom, we too have the capacity to grow, sometimes in ways that we didn't believe possible. Which leads us smoothly on to the next point: while Venus is the official ruler of Taurus (along with Libra), my late astrology teacher (a Taurus himself) believed that Mother Earth was actually more of an influencer for "The Bull" than Venus. Taurus, as a season and sign, is extremely impacted by its environment; it doesn't have the sort of ordered or clinical tidiness required by Virgo, but more of the "uncontrolled order" that is found in wild nature. Taurus is the most practical of signs. It is only really stimulated and nourished by tangible results and real solutions.

## Stabilizing the Divine Mother

If you have major Taurus stamps in your chart, the health of the Divine Mother directly impacts your own personal health and happiness. It impacts all of us, of course, as we all have a sprinkling of each sign somewhere.

So, let's all teach ourselves and others how to preserve the planet's health, while avoiding the urge to preach; our teaching must come from a place of compassion, not anger, otherwise we run the risk of closing hearts and minds rather than opening them. You may already know all of this and be doing all that you can to limit your own carbon footprint. If you are, know that you are making a huge difference and are loved and appreciated beyond words and worlds.

## The Power to Change

We do have the power to change ourselves and the world around us, but we must unite and make moves right now, for there is no sign, or time, as tenacious and resourceful as Taurus and Taurus season. For the next month at least, let's see what we can all do to make a difference. If we take public transportation whenever possible, if we stop supporting the production of fur and down clothing, if we support cruelty-free products and ditch the brands that still test on animals, we will force change upon the industries that already know that they have to change in the not too distant future. If we change our eating habits, that will have a massive impact. If you cannot resist eating dairy, meat or fish completely, just do so once a week, as a treat rather than a right. Try it this month. The future is now! It's in our own hands.

# Prophets over Profits

If we recycle, support consignment shops, don't buy stuff we don't need, use 100 percent recycled paper and buy wood from legal sources with an FSC stamp, we become prophets who refuse to encourage suffering for profits. No one is perfect, but if we all try a little harder, we will lift the blanket of depression currently covering us and the great Mother Earth.

You may think that all this has little to do with astrology, but it does. Astrology is an interpretation of energy and, as a coach, I like to figure out solutions to increase our contentment and connection. Also, astrology, when translated correctly, is the sacred language of the stars, and the stars and planets are trying to speak to us so that we may raise our awareness and consciousness in order to reconnect to the universal soul. We should listen to what they have to say and act accordingly. This will make us all happier.

# Retrograde Planets

This month begins the first major cycle of retrograde planets of 2020. Remember that retrogrades are not negative, they are simply a change in energy, and this can be used effectively if we know what signs are impacted in our chart.

With the current astrological activities, this month is brilliant for planning in general. I call Taurus "The Architect" of the zodiac, because behind the most beautiful buildings and fabulous gardens a drawing came first. Plan out your ideas, start with the end goal first and then map out what you will need to do to achieve that goal, then let the paint dry until the Sun moves into Gemini, giving some serious mental boosts to your fail-proof strategy!

*Taurus's mantra:* **I am present in the moment and plan for the future.**

# Friday, May 1st–
# Sunday, May 3rd

## Forecast

This week begins with the Sun and Mercury, the planet that governs communications, in the sign of Taurus, which is a gorgeous combination. If you stop and breathe for long enough, you can refresh your whole being with simple delights and an appreciation of life.

Venus, the planet of love and pleasures, is in the sign of Gemini, sparking an interest in fresh stimuli and also experiences brimming with opportunities to learn, socialize and meet exciting people.

## Mission

- Even though we have the steadying influence of the Sun and Mercury in Taurus now, we still have Mars in the sign of Aquarius, which can push us to keep going without realizing that we need to recharge our batteries, so use this weekend as a time to relax and be kind to yourself. Honor the "May Day" tradition and immerse yourself in flowers somehow.

- Meditate every morning for at least ten minutes. Make an opening and closing affirmation or just use the chant "Om."

- Buy a new plant or potted flower and research how to care for it. It gives you air, so give it a name and try to keep it alive.

- Relax and spend time in nature; hug a tree if you are feeling adventurous and breathe in its life-giving oxygen.

*Aspiration/mantra:* **I am a beautiful being.**

# Friday, May 1st

**May Day.**
The Moon is in Leo. This is a good day to put a spring into your step; walk as much as you can and try to smile and laugh, as there is nothing more refreshing than laughter.
Power surge for those with major stamps in Aquarius, Leo and Virgo.

**Mission completed?** Challenge level: 1–5: Ideas and insights:

_____

_____

# Saturday, May 2nd

The Moon moves into Virgo. Avoid stress by doing a few minutes of extra meditation and turning your phone off!

**Mission completed?** Challenge level: 1–5: Ideas and insights:

_____

_____

# Sunday, May 3rd

**Mission completed?** Challenge level: 1–5: Ideas and insights:

_____

_____

# Reflections ...

If you managed to complete this week's mission, how did it make you feel?

If you skipped anything, did you feel any different?

Are you feeling the nourishing Taurus vibes?

How did the weekend's aspiration unfold?

List a few things, or even just one, that you are grateful for.

Are there any takeaways from this week that you would like to address next week? Try reflecting without judgment.

# Monday, May 4th– Sunday, May 10th

## Forecast

Celebrate springtime! The Sun and Mercury are more aligned than they were last week and this will be a spectacular energy to tap into to work on your game plan for the week ahead. Asking which of your dreams hold value and what you wish to transform will produce nothing short of magic under the Scorpio Full Moon on Sunday.

When Taurus is strong, it's a smart move to review our eating habits and to avoid extremes. If you're not already fighting fit on all three levels (mind, body and spirit), then the start of this month will shoot arrows of inspiration to help you take the very first steady steps toward transformation. If you don't like something about yourself or your life, now is the time to make a plan: just remember that the very first step is the hardest. While under the Sun in Taurus's mighty glare, mapping out a simple and achievable plan is the best way to get started, and then so much can be achieved.

## Mission

- Meditate every day for at least ten minutes. Slow (or steady) your racing mind and train it with your breath to stay in the moment.

- Celebrate all of the people in your life who operate from a heart space. Tell one person each day (it can be by text!) how much you appreciate their generous heart! (You can send your message to yourself on one of the days.)

- Get creative with your menu planning and ask other people for suggestions. Try quitting meat, or, if not, sending some words of gratitude to the animals who have made a sacrifice for you. Remember, we must care for our mind and our body.

- Don't buy a single item that you don't need. If you slip up, donate something you already have to a charity shop.

*Aspiration/mantra:* **Spiritual growth.**

## Monday, May 4th

The Moon moves into Libra.
Power surge for those with major stamps in Capricorn and Libra.

**Mission completed?** Challenge level: 1–5: Ideas and insights:

## Tuesday, May 5th

**Cinco de Mayo.**
This is a wonderful opportunity to tune in to the magic of the Mexican culture. This festival originates from the day when the Mexican army, even though seriously outnumbered, managed to win a battle against the French army, in Puebla, on May, 5th 1862. Cinco de Mayo honors this and reminds us that when we are outnumbered but unite by putting heart and soul into something, even though it may take more than one lifetime, eventually we will win.

The North Node goes retrograde and switches sign to Gemini.

**Mission completed?** Challenge level: 1–5: Ideas and insights:

# Wednesday, May 6th

The Moon moves into Scorpio.
Power surge for those with major stamps in Capricorn and Scorpio.

**Mission completed?** Challenge level: 1–5: Ideas and insights:

---

# Thursday, May 7th

## Full Moon in Scorpio (5:45 AM EDT)

This Full Moon is perfect for releasing and transforming any negative experiences that may be holding you back from expressing your true self. Scorpio energy is the most potent to use for rituals, and when combined with the magnified power of a Full Moon, that is as good as it gets.

- Write down all of your heartaches and any traits that you wish to transform, telling that piece of paper your darkest fears and secrets.
- Then light some candles and burn the paper (safely!) and release all that is on it to the Moon Goddess in order to move on, rising from the flames like a phoenix.

**Mission completed?** Challenge level: 1–5: Ideas and insights:

---

# Friday, May 8th

The Moon moves into Sagittarius.
To feel fabulous on an emotional level, get out in nature as much as you can today and seek out friends and pastimes that lift your spirit and speak to your soul.
Power surge for those with major stamps in Capricorn and Sagittarius.

**Mission completed?** Challenge level: 1–5: Ideas and insights:

# Saturday, May 9th

**Mission completed?** Challenge level: 1–5: Ideas and insights:

# Sunday, May 10th

The Moon moves into Capricorn.
Power surge for those with major stamps in Aquarius and Capricorn.

**Mission completed?** Challenge level: 1–5: Ideas and insights:

# Reflections ...

If you managed to complete this week's mission, how did it make you feel?

_____

_____

If you skipped anything, did you feel any different?

_____

_____

Was the Full Moon intense? Did you complete your Full Moon ritual? If so, did you feel uplifted afterward?

_____

_____

How did the week's aspiration unfold?

_____

_____

List a few things, or even just one, that you are grateful for.

_____

_____

Are there any takeaways from this week that you would like to address next week? Try reflecting without judgment.

_____

_____

# Monday, May 11th–Sunday, May 17th

## Forecast

This is a big week for retrogrades! The North Node represents the karmic direction in which we are collectively heading. If it's matched with your own North Node in your birth chart, then you are in a period of time known as a "North Node Return" and this will be a seriously profound time. This week the North Node shifts from Cancer, giving those folks a little break, and into Gemini.

At this time you may meet people that you feel you have known before and have an unexplainably deep connection with, which is fantastic, but remember that soul connections are not always rose quartz crystals, so slow down and get to know who those souls are in this life! You may also be rewarded for all the good things that you have done in one lifetime or another. Saturn goes retrograde in Aquarius on Monday, and Venus goes retrograde in Gemini on Wednesday, so old flames and friends may reappear, perhaps to resolve issues. Gemini is about truth, and scratching the surface of what may be presented as "reality" to see what lies beneath. If you have any major stamps in Gemini or its opposite sign, Sagittarius, this influence will be particularly strong for you.

Mars moves into Pisces, so relax and try not to push too hard, though, as this is a better time for going with the creative and imaginative flow.

## Mission

- Meditate every morning and center yourself.
- If you get yourself a daily tea or coffee, buy a reusable cup.
- Try to quit dairy; be creative in finding "bad-karma-free" alternatives.

- Using the exercises below, open up your heart before you leave the house:
  - ○ Stand in what is known as Tadasana, mountain pose: center your feet firmly on the floor, close together with the heels slightly apart.
  - ○ Lift your toes and fan them out, then bring them back to the ground.
  - ○ Take a few deep breaths. On the inhale, your diaphragm should lift; on the exhale, you should make a sound like a mighty sigh.
  - ○ Inhale and sweep your arms up to the sky with your palms facing each other. Look up at your thumbs and take a few deep breaths. Take a gentle backbend.
  - ○ Exhale and bring your hands down to your heart in prayer position (Anjali Mudra).
  - ○ Repeat until you feel the flow of your energy has lifted.
  - ○ Say, "I am a being of light," or use your own affirmation if you prefer.

*Aspiration/mantra:* **I have good karma.**

## Monday, May 11th

Mercury moves into Gemini.
Saturn goes retrograde in Aquarius. This is quite positive, as it relaxes the Aquarian pressure and tames the rebellious streak. Those Aquarian vibes are pretty strong all year, so it's good to chill out for a while and let the dust settle! There's time now to build on ideas that have been buzzing around.

**Mission completed?** Challenge level: 1–5: Ideas and insights:

_____

_____

## Tuesday, May 12th

The Moon moves into Aquarius and, at the end of the day, it connects with Mars, so sleep without any electricity buzzing around you and you'll wake up feeling supercharged or have dreams that will help you to trip the light fantastic.
Power surge for those with major stamps in Capricorn and Aquarius.

**Mission completed?** Challenge level: 1–5: Ideas and insights:

## Wednesday, May 13th

Mars moves into Pisces.
Venus goes retrograde in Gemini. Old flames often resurface when Venus retrogrades, and friends that you may have lost touch with may re-enter your life. If you need to forgive them, do so, and be kind but firm with anyone who has been less than honest. Financial negotiations may slow down, but just be patient and view this as an opportunity to review all the finer details.

**Mission completed?** Challenge level: 1–5: Ideas and insights:

## Thursday, May 14th

Jupiter goes retrograde in Capricorn until September. This slows down the expansion of the Capricorn vibe and should give us all a little break from the constant feeling that we should be achieving more, both personally and professionally. Be in the moment, lighten up and enjoy this period of star-chill.
Power surge for those with major stamps in Taurus and Pisces.

**Mission completed?** Challenge level: 1–5: Ideas and insights:

_____

_____

# Friday, May 15th

The Moon moves into Pisces. It also connects with Mars in Pisces over the weekend, and so lethargy may kick in as you are encouraged to dip into your imagination and creativity. Play music, watch uplifting films, visit the ocean or spend time near other bodies of water if you can.

**Mission completed?** Challenge level: 1–5: Ideas and insights:

_____

_____

# Saturday, May 16th

**Mission completed?** Challenge level: 1–5: Ideas and insights:

_____

_____

# Sunday, May 17th

The Moon moves into Aries.
With Aries as the house, it's time to think about action plans once again. Be careful not to rush, or to make kneejerk decisions. This phase is brilliant for active sports and the like; not so hot for tolerance and patience.
Power surge for those with major stamps in Capricorn and Aries.

**Mission completed?** Challenge level: 1–5: Ideas and insights:

_____

_____

# Reflections ...

If you managed to complete this week's mission, how did it make you feel?

_____

_____

If you skipped anything, did you feel any different?

_____

_____

Have you noticed any difference with the retrograde planets yet?

_____

_____

How did the week's aspiration unfold? Did it help you to notice the real people that you encountered?

_____

_____

List a few things, or even just one, that you are grateful for.

_____

_____

Are there any takeaways from this week that you would like to address next week? Try reflecting without judgment.

# Monday, May 18th–
# Sunday, May 24th

## Forecast

The Sun moves into Gemini on Wednesday, which lightens up the energy for us all, but the week starts with the Moon in Taurus and this is a rather lovely combination. Make the most of it by encouraging playfulness and spending time with interesting people who nourish you.

The New Moon in Gemini on Friday is a perfect time to set your intentions for the next few weeks at least. Gemini energy is an incredible opportunity to think up new ideas and create award-worthy campaigns and strategies. There is a catch, though: it's only really worthwhile for those who can focus for long enough to see the ideas through. This week we need to train our mind to stay in one place and execute our ideas, otherwise the energy will fail to deliver any lasting results, but I have faith in you not to let this happen!

## Mission

Due to the distractions sent by the Gemini and Aquarius air-vibe and the general need to focus this week, I have upped the ante slightly in order to aid your success.

- Meditate every morning for fifteen minutes.

- Do not look at your phone until you have had a shower (or washed) and brushed your teeth.

- If you commute to work, take a book and read at least one chapter.

- Train your mind to stay in one place throughout the day: focus on a picture, or any image that fills you with happiness, and take a few deep breaths.

*Aspiration/mantra:* **I make good things happen.**

## Monday, May 18th

**Mission completed?** Challenge level: 1–5: Ideas and insights:

---

## Tuesday, May 19th

Power surge for those with major stamps in Capricorn and Taurus.

**Mission completed?** Challenge level: 1–5: Ideas and insights:

---

## Wednesday, May 20th

The Sun moves into Gemini.
The Moon moves into Taurus.

**Mission completed?** Challenge level: 1–5: Ideas and insights:

---

## Thursday, May 21st

**Mission completed?** Challenge level: 1–5: Ideas and insights:

_____

_____

## Friday, May 22nd

### New Moon in Gemini (12:39 PM EDT)

- Write a list of the things that you wish to manifest this month, and in your life generally.
- Imagine them happening and then burn the list and ask the universe to deliver for you.

Power surge for those with major stamps in Capricorn and Gemini.

**Mission completed?** Challenge level: 1–5: Ideas and insights:

_____

_____

## Saturday, May 23rd

**Mission completed?** Challenge level: 1–5: Ideas and insights:

_____

_____

## Sunday, May 24th

Power surge for those with major stamps in Gemini and Cancer.

**Mission completed?** Challenge level: 1–5: Ideas and insights:

_____

_____

# Reflections ...

If you managed to complete this week's mission, how did it make you feel?

_____

_____

If you skipped anything, did you feel any different?

_____

_____

Did you notice the change in energy when the Sun moved into Gemini?

_____

_____

Did you write a New Moon manifestation list?

_____

_____

How did the week's aspiration unfold? Did it help you to notice the real people that you encountered?

_____

_____

List a few things, or even just one, that you are grateful for.

_____

_____

Are there any takeaways from this week that you would like to address next week? Try reflecting without judgment.

_____

_____

# Monday, May 25th– Sunday, May 31st

## Forecast

The people that you encounter may be a tad more sensitive than usual this week, as we begin the week with the Moon in Cancer, the sign it governs. Both impact our emotions and the collective mood. And then Mercury, the sign of communication, moves into Cancer on Thursday. That's wonderful, if we can avoid taking outbursts or any snipes personally. If we handle people carefully and kindly, we will feel so great. Watch that you don't become overtired, as that's when you are likely to overreact.

## Mission

- Meditate every day, for ten minutes at least.
- Only speak kind words to yourself and others.
- Give your feet a treat: try some reflexology, or get your loved one to massage them with oils (or do it for yourself).
- Work on some hip-opening exercises in order to release stagnant emotional energy. You may do your own or follow this example daily:
  - Come onto all fours, also known in Yoga as "tabletop."
  - Lift one of your knees out to the side and gently draw circles with it as you breathe deeply. Use your core to power you and prevent you from straining your lower back.
  - Repeat on both sides for as many times as you can manage.

*Aspiration/mantra:* **I am sensitive and kind.**

## Monday, May 25th

The Moon moves into Cancer. Be kind to yourself and others today and make a concerted effort to hit "pause" if you feel as though you may react emotionally.

**Mission completed?** Challenge level: 1–5: Ideas and insights:

_____

_____

## Tuesday, May 26th

**Mission completed?** Challenge level: 1–5: Ideas and insights:

_____

_____

## Wednesday, May 27th

The Moon moves into Leo.
Power surge for those with major stamps in Capricorn and Leo.

**Mission completed?** Challenge level: 1–5: Ideas and insights:

_____

_____

## Thursday, May 28th

Mercury moves into Cancer. Re-read the weekly forecast!
Power surge for those with major stamps in Gemini and Virgo.

**Mission completed?** Challenge level: 1–5: Ideas and insights:

_____

_____

## Friday, May 29th

The Moon moves into Virgo.

**Mission completed?** Challenge level: 1–5: Ideas and insights:

_____

_____

## Saturday, May 30th

**Mission completed?** Challenge level: 1–5: Ideas and insights:

_____

_____

## Sunday, May 31st

The Moon moves into Libra.
Power surge for those with major stamps in Capricorn and Libra.

**Mission completed?** Challenge level: 1–5: Ideas and insights:

_____

_____

# Reflections ...

If you managed to complete this week's mission, how did it make you feel?

_____

_____

If you skipped anything, did you feel any different?

Did you notice any overtly emotional energy? How did you handle it?

How did the week's aspiration unfold? Did it help you to notice the real people that you encountered?

List a few things, or even just one, that you are grateful for. This is a powerful indicator to the universe that you are aware of its blessings.

Are there any takeaways from this week that you would like to address next week? Try reflecting without judgment.

Take a few moments to applaud yourself. Even if you only completed one part of the mission, that's still progress!

# June

June is believed to have been named after the Roman goddess Juno, who was Jupiter's wife and the goddess of marriage. In your full birth chart, you will find Juno, and it represents the kind of traits and qualities (by sign) that you will need to attract in a partner to cultivate the right marriage for you – if, indeed, that is what you want! Marriage here is not just about a holy matrimony, it is also indicative of those you will commit to professionally. A wise man once told me that it was probably easier to get out of a bad marriage than a bad business union. So, we need to do due diligence before we commit to anyone or anything. Finding out where our Juno is will help.

## Signs in the Spotlight

*Gemini* (also its opposite sign, *Sagittarius*, to a lesser degree, until the Full Moon in Sagittarius on June 5th).

*Pisces* (also its opposite sign, *Virgo*, to a lesser degree).

*Cancer* (also its opposite sign, *Capricorn*, to a lesser degree).

# The Month of Youth and Storytellers

"June" is also thought to have derived from the Latin word *iuniores*, which means "young." Anyone who has major stamps in Gemini or is an actual Gemini will be likely to have a light and youthful approach to life and a subtle, mischievous streak that never fails to stave off boredom. This vibe is all around us for the next few weeks and it's so important that we lighten up and take everything sincerely but not too seriously! Gemini, as a time and sign, is not one to be morosely deep or brooding; it prefers to use wit and intelligence to spark the art of interesting debate, and "gone right"; it abhors stupidity and ignorance. All these traits are shared with its opposite sign, Sagittarius. Both signs, at times, may lack tact and tolerance, and sometimes even enjoy playing tricks on unsuspecting others, simply to stay amused. Smart and sassy Gemini season is refreshing, though, and we all have the capacity right now to dial into this vibe and channel Gemini's unrivaled skill for storytelling.

Gemini is also the sign and the time of the thinker, the mind and the rationale. We can all educate ourselves; education is the great equalizer.

Gemini people have used the power of the mind, and word, in many ways. Irwin Allen Ginsberg, who was born in June, used the written word to oppose materialism and oppression. His best-known poem, *Howl*, was seized in 1956 by police in San Francisco because it openly described not only heterosexual but also homosexual relationships. Ginsberg, who was one of the fathers of the counterculture revolution, preferred to live modestly, buying his clothes in thrift stores and practising Buddhism. He was a student of the incredible Tibetan master Chögyam Trungpa, who escaped Tibet in 1959, when it was occupied by Chinese armed forces. He was one of only a few who managed to survive, including my late, great teacher Akong Choje Tulku Rinpoche. All of them initially sought refuge in India and then the West. Akong Rinpoche founded the first Tibetan monastery in the rolling hills of Scotland (Samye-Ling). Chögyam Trungpa became famous for his radical representation of the "Shambala" vision, the idea that every human being has a fundamental nature of basic goodness. He set up his headquarters in Boulder, Colorado, and founded the Naropa Institute, which was the first accredited University of Buddhism in America.

If the Chinese invasion hadn't happened, we would have been unlikely to have ever had such enlightened teachings in the West, teachings that remind us of the importance of meditation as an example of spiritual practice, of raising awareness and the benefits of retreat and the necessity of loving kindness. And in Chinese the word for "crisis" also means "opportunity" …

I sometimes think that so many people in the West have lost their spirituality because here we do not have unbroken spiritual lineages, and the higher religious powers are reluctant to accept the possibility that our great spiritual prophets have probably reincarnated many, many times over. Our faith needs to awaken, adapt and be all-inclusive.

# Gemini: The Sign and Time of Communication

Words are Gemini's weapon of choice and, as we all know, they can be used with bad intentions or simply to produce incredulity. This month we are tasked with mastering our communications: thoughts, words and exchanges:

- Allowing ourselves to speak unkindly to our fragile heart is something that needs to end now. We need to pause, take hold of our tongue if cruel words are on the tip of it and change any low-vibe thoughts and speech. It's a simple life hack that can unlock inner happiness.

- We live with our mind 24/7, 365 days a year, so it's wise to make friends with that, too, and be kind to it!

# Purpose and Belonging

Being active, as Gemini often is, means being concerned about the welfare of others and the planet and trying to do our bit to alleviate the suffering of both. It fills us with a deep sense of purpose and belonging in this often lonely world, where our lives can be brimming with friends and activities yet we can still feel lonely if we have lost our soul connection with one other and to the Great Mother. Let's make a pact to get that connection back!

Once again, you may wonder what this has to do with astrology. Remember, this is Dynamic Astrology™. "Dynamic," as an adjective, defines a certain kind of energy or effective action, while as a noun it is something that motivates or brings about development and stability. In order to stabilize ourselves, we have to have a stable environment, and we all share the same home, Earth, so caring for it naturally follows on.

# Retrogrades Galore

This year, June is overloaded with retrograde planetary activity; in fact the only planet that remains steady and direct is Uranus, in the sign of Taurus (figures!). Uranus is the great awakener, and also triggers seemingly mad inventions that offer incredibly sane solutions.

As for the retrogrades, Mercury goes retrograde in Cancer on June 18th and stays that way until July 10th; Venus is retrograde in the sign of Gemini up until June 25th; Jupiter and Pluto are retrograde in Capricorn until September and October, respectively; Saturn is retrograde in Aquarius until July and then remains retrograde, shifting back into Capricorn until December. There's a lot going on!

So, what does all of this mean for us? I will go into more detail in the weekly and daily summaries, but for the most part, it's all about reviewing aspects of our life. Retrogrades give us the chance to reflect and make mandatory amendments, while asking us to consider what is meaningful to us. June is the time for reaching deep inside our heart and extracting the deeper truths, especially when we celebrate the Full Moon's release in the sign of Sagittarius on the 5th. Time for the lies to subside, particularly the ones that we tell ourselves!

*Gemini's mantra:* **I am interesting and interested.**

# Monday, June 1st– Sunday, June 7th

## Forecast

The Sun is shining brightly in the sign of Gemini, which gives anyone with major stamps in this sign a major boost.

The next week is not particularly well starred for action, because the planet of action, Mars, is in Pisces, and the latter fuels the world of the intangible, as opposed to that of reality. This is not to say that we cannot achieve anything worldly, it just means that we need to go with the flow, revise goals and plans, and be gentle and kind to ourselves and each other.

This is a marvelous week to write and create and also to read for inspiration. We may feel a little more sensitive than usual, so avoiding loud or aggressive people is advised in order to give ourselves the space that we need to connect with the deeper aspects of our mind. The Full Moon is major on Friday: it's in Sagittarius, so it may push us to delve deep and search for our own truth. Use this Moon phase as a moment to release anything that is other than authentic.

We start the week with Say Something Nice Day. This is a tradition which was initiated by the mayors and other townsfolk of Charleston, South Carolina, in 2006, and I believe that we should roll it out globally! Gemini season shines a spotlight on communications as a whole, so let's begin the month as we mean to go on!

## Mission

- Training the mind begins within, so continue with your morning meditation:
  - ○ Sit quietly in the same spot with crossed legs.

○ Close your eyes and breathe deeply. On the inhale, fill your tummy with air. Hold for a few seconds.

○ Gently exhale any tension.

● In addition to this, every day, try to catch hold of yourself before something unkind trips out of your mouth or takes root inside your mind. Take a deep breath and change it to something nice. If someone is being unkind to you, or to themselves, then be gentle and assertive and repeat to yourself: "Now say something nice."

*Aspiration/mantra:* **Say something nice.**

## Monday, June 1st

**Say Something Nice Day.**
Try saying something kind to someone, but make sure it's genuine. Perhaps tell someone with whom you have had conflict that you are sorry, or offer kind words to someone who is serving you, such as "Thanks, I appreciate that," which, in real terms, means "You are not faceless. I see you!"

The Moon is in Libra. This is the perfect Moon phase to increase harmony and peace.

**Mission completed?** Challenge level: 1–5: Ideas and insights:

## Tuesday, June 2nd

The Moon moves into Scorpio. Focus on forgiveness today: forgive a person who has upset you or offended you. That includes yourself. If we hold on to grudges, we become stuck in the past: the past is an illusion and nothing progressive will come from remaining there.
Power surge for those with stamps in Scorpio and Capricorn.

**Mission completed?** Challenge level: 1–5: Ideas and insights:

## Wednesday, June 3rd

**Mission completed?** Challenge level: 1–5: Ideas and insights:

## Thursday, June 4th

The Moon moves into Sagittarius.
Power surge for those with stamps in Sagittarius and Capricorn.

**Mission completed?** Challenge level: 1–5: Ideas and insights:

## Friday, June 5th

### Full Moon in Sagittarius (2:12 PM EDT)

Partial lunar eclipse

- This is the perfect time to review what is true for you and write down all that you believe about yourself and those close to you. Try not to be too critical, but if you are, counteract this with something kind soon after. Ask yourself: "What is my truth?"

- Reflect, then burn the list and meditate for a little while with some lit candles and cushions.

**National Doughnut Day.**
This day succeeded the doughnut event started by the Salvation Army in Chicago in 1938 to honor their members who served doughnuts to soldiers during the First World War. So, why not donate a doughnut to someone in honor of the Salvation Army and their little "sweet treat" gestures of kindness.

**Mission completed?** Challenge level: 1–5: Ideas and insights:

## Saturday, June 6th

The Moon moves into Capricorn.
The North Node goes direct in Gemini.
Power surge for those with stamps in Pisces and Capricorn.

**Mission completed?** Challenge level: 1–5: Ideas and insights:

_____

_____

## Sunday, June 7th

On this day in 1979 President Jimmy Carter initiated African American Music Appreciation Month. Play some music, listen to some bands and fill your home and workspace with uplifting music that speaks to the soul.

**Mission completed?** Challenge level: 1–5: Ideas and insights:

_____

_____

# Reflections ...

If you managed to complete this week's mission, how did it make you feel?

_____

_____

If you skipped anything, did you feel any different?

_____

_____

Did you notice feeling any different when the Full Moon was in Sagittarius?

_____

_____

Did you write a list and contemplate your truth?

_____

_____

How did the week's aspiration unfold? Did it help you change conversations?

_____

_____

Did you manage to say something nice each day?

_____

_____

List a few things, or even just one, that you are grateful for.

_____

_____

Are there any takeaways from this week that you would like to address next week? Try reflecting without judgment.

_____

_____

# Monday, June 8th– Sunday, June 14th

## Forecast

We celebrate World Oceans Day on Monday, so this week is a time to avoid all plastic and to quit eating fish; Neptune, the ruler of Pisces and god of the seas, wishes to be heard. Both Neptune and Mars are in the sign of Pisces, making this the perfect moment for us to take visionary action. By the time the Moon moves in to join them on Thursday, we will have a feeling of hope and faith in our heart, simply from knowing that, even just for one week, thousands of us will be doing our bit for the oceans. Neptune will no doubt reward this and, as we purify our diets and habits, a feeling of connection and oneness will inspire us no end.

The North Node, which indicates the collective karmic direction in which we are heading, is retrograde this week, in Gemini, and this asks that we slow down and stop engaging with the distractions that prevent us from embracing deeper meaning in our life.

## Mission

In addition to ten minutes of daily meditation, this week is one for training your mind to focus, not allowing it to swerve so easily or hop to something that distracts you, even if you are less than excited by what's in front of you. But see your tasks through until you can tick them off. Here's your mission:

- Avoid eating any fish or seafood.

- Boycott plastic. When you buy food, go for something without any plastic packaging. Focus on attracting authenticity; avoid plastic/fake people.

- Buy a reusable flask or cup. If you already have one, buy one for your boss or a colleague when you go on the tea or coffee run.

*Aspiration/mantra:* **Boycott plastic.**

# Monday, June 8th

**World Oceans Day.**
Power surge for those with stamps in Aquarius and Capricorn.

**Mission completed?** Challenge level: 1–5: Ideas and insights:

---

# Tuesday, June 9th

The Moon moves into Aquarius.

**Mission completed?** Challenge level: 1–5: Ideas and insights:

---

# Wednesday, June 10th

Power surge for those with stamps in Gemini and Pisces.

**Mission completed?** Challenge level: 1–5: Ideas and insights:

---

## Thursday, June 11th

The Moon moves into Pisces.

**Mission completed?** Challenge level: 1–5: Ideas and insights:

## Friday, June 12th

The North Node in Gemini goes retrograde. This is a signal for us to go beneath the surface and not to accept "fact" as anything other than theory, until we have checked for ourselves using reliable sources.

**Mission completed?** Challenge level: 1–5: Ideas and insights:

## Saturday, June 13th

The Moon moves into Aries.
Power surge for those with stamps in Aries and Capricorn.

**Mission completed?** Challenge level: 1–5: Ideas and insights:

## Sunday, June 14th

**Mission completed?** Challenge level: 1–5: Ideas and insights:

# Reflections ...

If you managed to complete this week's mission, how did it make you feel?

If you skipped anything, did you feel any different?

Did you boycott plastic? Did you notice how much of it is unnecessary?

How did the week's aspiration unfold? Did it help you?

List a few things, or even just one, that you are grateful for.

Are there any takeaways from this week that you would like to address next week? Try reflecting without judgment.

# Monday, June 15th– Sunday, June 21st

## Forecast

This week is well poised to be interesting and upbeat, as we have a really steadying connection between Uranus and the Moon in Taurus on Tuesday and Wednesday. This empowers our ability to be pragmatic and resourceful. Mercury in Cancer flips to its retrograde phase on Thursday, changing the vibe somewhat. It's vital that we don't become emotionally isolated or defensive, taking everything very personally.

There is the potential for us to really align with our intuition, though, especially as the Sun moves into Cancer on Saturday. We also have the New Moon in Cancer on Sunday, and a solar eclipse. Emotions and feelings are magnified under this influence and we will have an opportunity to enhance our emotional intelligence. If you allow yourself the freedom to be sensitive, while remaining optimistic and forgiving, you will really enjoy this combination. Being sensitive is a wonderful thing: embrace your sensitivity and match it with wisdom.

## Mission

- Please continue with your daily morning meditation, for at least ten minutes or more, if you can:
  - Sit quietly, cross-legged and straight-backed.
  - Close your eyes and take slow and steady deep breaths for ten minutes. Keep your mind in one place.
  - Inhale and extend your arms out to the side, palms facing up. Exhale, sweep your arms up, palms together, and look up at your thumbs.
  - Repeat gracefully until you feel refreshed.

- Now follow it up with this exercise:
  - ○ Pop your arms behind your back and clasp your hands together.
  - ○ Inhale and bring your shoulders forward. Exhale and bring your shoulders backward; imagine your heart opening and your shoulder blades trying to meet behind your back.
  - ○ Repeat.

*Aspiration/mantra:* **Honor sensitivity.**

# Monday, June 15th

**Mission completed?** Challenge level: 1–5: Ideas and insights:

---

---

# Tuesday, June 16th

The Moon moves into Taurus.
Uranus in Taurus connects with the Moon.
Power surge for those with stamps in Taurus and Capricorn.

**Mission completed?** Challenge level: 1–5: Ideas and insights:

---

---

## Wednesday, June 17th

**Mission completed?** Challenge level: 1–5: Ideas and insights:

## Thursday, June 18th

The Moon moves into Gemini.
Mercury retrogrades in Cancer.
Power surge for those with stamps in Gemini and Capricorn.

**Mission completed?** Challenge level: 1–5: Ideas and insights:

## Friday, June 19th

The North Node in Gemini goes direct.

**Mission completed?** Challenge level: 1–5: Ideas and insights:

# Saturday, June 20th

The Sun moves into Cancer.
The North Node in Gemini goes retrograde.
Power surge for those with stamps in Pisces and Cancer.

**Mission completed?** Challenge level: 1–5: Ideas and insights:

---

# Sunday, June 21st

## New Moon in Cancer at (2:12 PM EDT)

**Annular solar eclipse (2:41 AM EDT)**

A solar eclipse can only happen on a New Moon, when the Moon passes between the Earth and the Sun, blocking out most of the Sun's light and just leaving an outer ring for us to see. Because the Sun offers us light and impacts our ego and self-identity, this could result in us feeling low on energy and in mood. Try to avoid making life-changing decisions under this phase and focus on creativity and generosity instead.

This is the end of a cycle for Cancer and Capricorn and the start of something entirely new.

The Summer Solstice in the northern hemisphere – the longest day of the year. The Winter Solstice in the southern hemisphere – the shortest day of the year. Join celebrations today, no matter where you are, or your faith, and take part in positive, light-bringing rituals using prayer and fire.

**Mission completed?** Challenge level: 1–5: Ideas and insights:

_____

_____

# Reflections ...

If you managed to complete this week's mission, how did it make you feel?

_____

_____

If you skipped anything, did you feel any different?

_____

_____

How was Mercury retrograde for you? Did you notice anything different?

_____

_____

Did the energy change for you when the Sun moved to Cancer?

_____

_____

Did you write a manifestation list on the New Moon?

_____

_____

Did you notice the solar eclipse? How did you feel?

How did the week's aspiration unfold? Did it help you? Did you honor your sensitivity?

List a few things, or even just one, that you are grateful for.

Are there any takeaways from this week that you would like to address next week? Try reflecting without judgment.

# Monday, June 22nd– Sunday, June 28th

## Forecast

We begin the week with the Moon in Leo. This is always a great opportunity to embrace people, and projects, with heart. Even any difficult situations that arise can be smoothed over with lightness and humor. Neptune in Pisces goes retrograde until November; this can be challenging for all of us sensitive people, as we may feel a little off-key, or even lost, and are likely to be even more receptive to the suffering of the planet and our oceans. This is especially true for those with major stamps in Pisces. Don't feel despondent; do what you can and seek refuge in spiritual practice if you have a go-to one. If you don't, seek one out and connect to your higher mind.

Venus brings some lightness on Thursday, as it goes direct in Gemini, which brings more ease to negotiations and contractual agreements. When Venus connects to the North Node in Gemini at the latter end of the week, past karmic connections are likely to reappear in the guise of old flames, or we may encounter people that we feel we have known in a past life, which is always interesting, if not a little dangerous! Then there is a massive energy boost at the end of the week as Mars moves into its home sign of Aries.

## Mission

- Meditate every day for at least ten minutes. Just sit quietly and breathe deeply until you have prevented your mind from jumping around like a monkey.

- Immerse yourself in art. Join an art or craft class and learn the basics. If you already draw, paint or write, choose another medium.

*Aspiration/mantra:* **Take refuge in a higher vision.**

## Monday, June 22nd

**Mission completed?** Challenge level: 1–5: Ideas and insights:

_____

_____

## Tuesday, June 23rd

The Moon moves into Leo.
Neptune retrogrades in Pisces.
Power surge for those with stamps in Pisces and Leo.

**Mission completed?** Challenge level: 1–5: Ideas and insights:

_____

_____

## Wednesday, June 24th

Power surge for those with stamps in Taurus and Virgo.

**Mission completed?** Challenge level: 1–5: Ideas and insights:

_____

_____

## Thursday, June 25th

Venus goes direct in Gemini.
The Moon moves into Virgo.

**Mission completed?** Challenge level: 1–5: Ideas and insights:

_____

_____

## Friday, 26th June

**Mission completed?** Challenge level: 1–5: Ideas and insights:

_____

_____

## Saturday, June 27th

The Moon moves into Libra.
The North Node in Gemini goes direct.
Power surge for those with stamps in Pisces and Libra.

**Mission completed?** Challenge level: 1–5: Ideas and insights:

_____

_____

## Sunday, June 28th

Mars moves into Aries.

**Mission completed?** Challenge level: 1–5: Ideas and insights:

_____

_____

# Reflections ...

If you managed to complete this week's mission, how did it make you feel?

_____

_____

If you skipped anything, did you feel any different?

When Neptune began its retrograde motion did you feel any different?

Did you find or sign up for any artistic classes or creative outlets?

Did you notice when Mars moved into Aries on Sunday?

How did the week's aspiration unfold? Did it help you?

List a few things, or even just one, that you are grateful for.

Are there any takeaways from this week that you would like to address next week? Try reflecting without judgment.

# Monday, June 29th–
# Tuesday, June 30th

## Forecast

On Sunday we received a huge boost of energy from Mars. This particularly impacted those with major stamps in Aries but actually impacted us all. In the early part of this week, while it is giving us the drive to go and get what we want, it may also make us argumentative, or prone to attract this behavior from others, so be aware of this and proceed with caution and patience, especially on Monday, when the Moon is in Scorpio. That's a good time to focus on passion projects and people, but watch out for obsessive behavior.

## Mission

- Meditate every day for at least ten minutes. Just sit quietly and breathe deeply. Focus on the inhale and exhale, and if your mind wanders, do not chastise yourself, simply start again and stay calm.

- If you begin to obsess over something or someone, or feel anger, imagine the person or situation in front of you, then draw a circle around them and one around yourself, until you are in a "figure eight." Breathe deeply and cut the middle with imaginary scissors, then repeat the following: "I am no longer attached to this. I let this go with love. May the universe step in."

*Aspiration/mantra:* **This too shall pass.**

## Monday, June 29th

The Moon moves into Scorpio. Channel passion, not aggression. Power surge for those with stamps in Scorpio and Capricorn.

**Mission completed?** Challenge level: 1–5: Ideas and insights:

_____

_____

## Tuesday, June 30th

Jupiter and Pluto are in exact conjunction in Capricorn. This is great for commitments in general, and any opportunities or deals that arise over the next few days are likely to be important and have long-term implications. Choose wisely, stay positive and don't get sucked into superficial endeavors.

**Mission completed?** Challenge level: 1–5: Ideas and insights:

_____

_____

# Reflections ...

If you managed to complete this week's mission, how did it make you feel?

_____

_____

If you skipped anything, did you feel any different?

_____

_____

How did the week's aspiration unfold? Did it help you?

_____

_____

List a few things, or even just one, that you are grateful for.

_____

_____

Are there any takeaways from this week that you would like to address next week? Try reflecting without judgment.

_____

_____

Congratulate yourself for all efforts; now relax before you turn the page to July.

_____

_____

# July

❉

Welcome to July, also known as Cancer season, the time when we all embrace our sensitive, kind and fabulously creative natures. Some people believe that they are perhaps too sensitive, and indeed it can be a cross to bear, but this is only when sensitivity's not used alongside wisdom. When used positively, it is a wonderful trait. Cancer, the sign and time, is all about learning personal and collective energy management and knowing when and how to care for our well-being.

"July" was the name given to the seventh month by the Roman Senate in honor of their leader, Julius Caesar, who was born in this month.

This month we celebrate Independence Day. Many hail July 4th, the date on which the US declared independence from Britain, as the country's birthday, which would make it born under the sign of Cancer, but Cancer isn't the US's official star sign and I believe that July 4th was more like a rebirth. Christopher Columbus is credited with having discovered the Americas on October 12, 1492, which gives the US as we know it today a Sun sign of Libra, with the Moon in Cancer, five major stamps in Scorpio and Saturn in Aquarius. So, you could say that the Americas are in the midst of a rather major Saturn Return.

While it's now a date celebrated with fireworks and parties, the history of Independence Day runs deep, and, as is typical of the sign and time of Cancer, people died for their families, homes and country. Cancer is a sign and time that is focused on security, family and stability. It is a wonderfully nurturing sign, unless someone or something threatens the sanctity of its perception of family or security. Then you will arouse an unforgiving enemy far more dangerous than Scorpio "gone wrong," which is the sign usually deemed to be the most vengeful.

In the UK in the sixteenth century, Queen Elizabeth I was rightly concerned with her own personal security, and she regularly consulted the stars via astrologers,

John Dee in particular. She was a Virgo, and they fear vulnerability above all else, and she was crowned when the Sun was in Capricorn, the opposite sign to Cancer and the sign that rules royalty, tradition, status and ultimate governance!

# Signs in the Spotlight

*Cancer* (also its opposite sign, *Capricorn*, to a lesser degree, until the Full Moon in Capricorn on July 5th).

*Gemini* (also its opposite sign, *Sagittarius*, to a lesser degree).

*Aries* (also its opposite sign, *Libra*, to a lesser degree).

# Feeling Safe and Secure

We need to feel safe and secure, and Cancer as a time and as a sign makes us vulnerable to situations and people that will rattle our inner security until we have worked on steadying our own ship. We often feel most insecure when we think we need something or someone, so we can work on creating security for ourselves by working hard and being creative, but as long as we still "need" the approval and recognition of others, we will never truly be coming from a place of strength. We all need human connections, of course, but we should be considered in our approach and only accept a request to connect from someone who has a good heart.

This month is interesting, as the Sun is in Cancer, yet it's opposed by Pluto in Capricorn, which asks for changes that boost our emotional well-being and increase our overall emotional intelligence. It also asks that we review our thoughts relating to our need for security and our attitude to community. Anyone with major stamps in either sign will be forced to reassess the way that they make money as well as their commitments to safety.

Mars in Aries throughout the month will help us to achieve a lot if we can adopt patience and marry that with dynamism – not traits usually found in tandem, but when they are used skilfully, the results are superlative.

Taking others' needs into consideration is vital this month and beyond, especially after July 22nd, when the Sun moves into Leo, the sign that expands heart energy when it's working well and selfishness when it's not. Sticking to these rules will ensure that we are starred to succeed and that when we attempt to build or create anything nourishing and sustainable then the results will cater to our needs.

# Being Too Kind

Attitudes and thoughts are living things that roll out and create our reality. This month's missions will reflect this and help us all to train our thoughts and thus potentially change our life. Cancer, as a sign and time, is all about kindness. When people are mean or unkind, it is only because deep down they are unhappy. This is no excuse for bad behavior, or reason to accept it from others, but knowing it helps us to become kinder and more loving in our responses.

We also need to be kinder to ourselves. We must speak nicely to ourselves and take the time to build our inner security on a foundation of true acceptance. While none of us is perfect, if you were attracted to this journal it means that you are trying to be a better person, and that is all you need to do right now.

So, be kind, and know that there is no such thing as being too kind. When you hear others saying they were too kind, it means that they "gave" with the expectation of receiving something in return, and that is not truly giving. That is a transaction and isn't actually coming from an authentic place. To give without expectations is seriously difficult, but, once you become aware of those expectations, it will help you to shift perspective and to become stronger and more self-aware in the process. Saying "no" is also powerful: saying no to anything or anyone that makes you feel anything other than empowered will take you a long way.

# Wisdom and Strategy

The need for Cancer to protect itself is strong, and the only way to really protect ourselves is to learn how to cater for our own needs and manage our energy. The missions this month aim to do both these things. This month, more than ever, we have to master the art of self-care without throwing anyone else's needs out of the window in the process.

Venus is in Gemini all month. Gemini "gone right" is the sign most skilled in strategy, and this combination brings a smart, lighter and more playful vibe to the arena, as Venus governs the collective and individual heart and Gemini is all about communication. So, think and speak with your heart and watch out for overreactions triggered by the Sun and Mercury in Cancer crashing into all of the Capricorn planets mentioned above. Hit "pause" and think before you overshare in situations that are simply not appropriate. Many people believe that openness is the right way to operate, but lowering our guard and opening up to everyone can disempower us and erode the spiritual aura of protection that we all have. There is an art to being open and protected, and it's one that we need to learn this month and beyond; indeed, throughout our life if we have major Cancer stamps in our chart.

# Mercury Retrograde in Cancer

Mercury is retrograde in Cancer until July 12th. This can go right or very wrong. Mercury governs the collective mind and it's important that we influence this with our high-vibe thoughts and loving kindness. "Gone wrong" Mercury retrograde in Cancer makes people snappy, miserly, grasping, defensive and always ready to attack. Opening our heart is the best form of protection here, as a closed heart leads to bitterness, which acts as a repellent. Let's all stay beautiful and manage our energy this month by directing it into positive projects and people and knowing how to take care of ourselves.

*Cancer's mantra:* **I am safe and protected.**

# Wednesday, July 1st– Sunday, July 5th

## Forecast

These few days are packed with celestial activity: Saturn leaves Aquarius until December, it retrogrades to join Pluto and Jupiter in Capricorn, and we have a partial lunar eclipse and Full Moon in Capricorn on Sunday. Capricorn is all about mastery, and it's working with Cancer, which is all about emotions. So, try not to take anything too personally this week. Before you react, ask yourself if it really matters, and give yourself a huge gold star at the end of the week.

World UFO Day is celebrated on July 2nd (though some celebrate on June 24th, when aviator Kenneth Arnold reported what is considered to be the first UFO sighting). The July date commemorates the famed incident in July 1947, when a UFO was reported to have crashed just outside Roswell, New Mexico; the incident was then apparently covered up by the government. In 1973, when Jimmy Carter was a senator in Georgia, he officially reported having seen a UFO in 1969 and swore that if he ever became president, he would request that the CIA release to the public all of the UFO files that they had. After he was elected president in 1976, however, he said that it was not in the interests of national security to do so. Perhaps he was right. It's a complex issue. There have been many reports of UFO sightings, some dating back to the time of the pharaohs, and a lot of money has been spent trying to seek proof of the existence of intelligent life on planets beyond our own. Personally, I don't think I have ever seen a UFO. But I sometimes think that aliens walk among us anyway! There is so much that we do not know, so it's prudent to keep an open mind and keep calm and carry on regardless.

# Mission

Ten minutes of meditation along with a little mind training:

- Sit quietly for ten minutes with your eyes closed and take deep breaths.

- Try to avoid moving your body apart from the rise and fall of your breath.

- Allow the in-breath to nourish you. Allow the out-breath to release any anxiety.

- Recognize any negative thoughts passing through your mind, then pause and change them to positive ones.

- Each day, make a note of each time that you manage to do this and give yourself a pat on the back. Even managing this once a day is a real achievement!

- Count the times that you changed your thoughts each day and add up the total at the end of the week.

*Aspiration/mantra:* **I am in charge of my thoughts and feelings.**

## Wednesday, July 1st

The Moon is in Scorpio.
Saturn goes retrograde and moves into Capricorn. Today is all about self-mastery and restraint. Honor your feelings but avoid allowing them to run wild. Power surge for those with stamps in Scorpio, Sagittarius and Capricorn.

**Mission completed?** Challenge level: 1–5: Ideas and insights:

------

------

## Thursday, July 2nd

**World UFO Day.**
The Moon moves into Sagittarius.

**Mission completed?** Challenge level: 1–5: Ideas and insights:

_____

_____

## Friday, July 3rd

Power surge for those with stamps in Pisces and Capricorn.

**Mission completed?** Challenge level: 1–5: Ideas and insights:

_____

_____

## Saturday, July 4th

The Moon moves into Capricorn.

**Mission completed?** Challenge level: 1–5: Ideas and insights:

_____

_____

## Sunday, 5th July

### Full Moon in Capricorn (12:44 AM EDT)

Partial lunar eclipse. It's ritual time!

- Write down all the negative thoughts that you have about yourself, your career and your relationships, along with your fears.

- Burn the list and ask the universe to dissolve these issues for you.

- Be ready to focus on healing and appreciating all that you are and all that you have achieved so far in life.

**Mission completed?** Challenge level: 1–5: Ideas and insights:

# Reflections ...

If you managed to complete this week's mission, how did it make you feel?

If you skipped anything, did you feel any different?

Did you feel different when the Full Moon was in Capricorn?

_____

_____

Did you write a list and release negative thoughts?

_____

_____

How did the week's aspiration unfold? Did it help you to change conversations?

_____

_____

Did you manage to change negative thoughts each day?

_____

_____

List a few things, or even just one, that you are grateful for.

_____

_____

Are there any takeaways from this week that you would like to address next week? Try reflecting without judgment.

_____

_____

# Monday, July 6th–
# Sunday, July 12th

## Forecast

This week His Holiness the Dalai Lama celebrates his birthday, and there is no better public role model of living with compassion and loving kindness. Compassion is aspirational, as it cannot be truly authentic unless we have mastered the art of non-attachment (it's not so hard to be compassionate toward people that we like or have pity for). This week asks us to try to feel compassion for those that we find annoying or dislike. Cancer season works best when everyone practices kindness, and this will be even more powerful at the start of the week, when the Moon is in the sign of Aquarius – Aquarius being the sign that has the ability to evoke compassion. Most of us know that when people behave badly they plant seeds of negative karma that will grow in their life, but we must try to have compassion for them rather than taking solace in the fact that, at some point, they will face the music. Compassion for ignorance is key.

Mercury goes direct on Sunday and this will enable us to alter our schedules accordingly and spend time on projects and people we really care about.

## Mission

Ten minutes of meditation along with a little more mind training:

- Sit quietly for ten minutes or more each morning.
- Imagine breathing in white light that envelops your whole body. Exhale stress and anxiety.
- Notice when you feel low on energy and breathe the white rejuvenating light into your whole being.

- Hold your negative thoughts, thank them and then flip them into the positive. For example, when someone is being annoying, instead of allowing words of discord to fill your mind, say: "This person radiates with joy and light," or even "This person is my teacher."

*Aspiration/mantra:* **I practice loving kindness.**

## Monday, July 6th

The Moon moves into Aquarius. Turn up the tolerance.
Power surge for those with stamps in Aquarius and Capricorn.

**Mission completed?** Challenge level: 1–5: Ideas and insights:

## Tuesday, July 7th

Power surge for those with stamps in Taurus and Pisces.

**Mission completed?** Challenge level: 1–5: Ideas and insights:

## Wednesday, July 8th

The Moon moves into Pisces. Time to evoke the inner artist. Avoid negative, escapist behavior and tune in to your intuitive and gentle nature. Be creative.

**Mission completed?** Challenge level: 1–5: Ideas and insights:

## Thursday, July 9th

**Mission completed?** Challenge level: 1–5: Ideas and insights:

## Friday, July 10th

**Mission completed?** Challenge level: 1–5: Ideas and insights:

## Saturday, July 11th

The Moon moves into Aries.
Power surge for those with stamps in Aries and Capricorn.

**Mission completed?** Challenge level: 1–5: Ideas and insights:

## Sunday, July 12th

Mercury goes direct in Cancer. It's a day to take care of yourself and those you consider "family." Be kind to yourself and others without any expectations.

**Mission completed?** Challenge level: 1–5: Ideas and insights:

_____

_____

# Reflections ...

If you managed to complete this week's mission, how did it make you feel?

_____

_____

If you skipped anything, did you feel any different?

_____

_____

How did the week's aspiration unfold? Were you more loving and kinder?

_____

_____

How was the white-light tip?

_____

_____

Did you manage to change negative thoughts each day?

List a few things, or even just one, that you are grateful for.

Are there any takeaways from this week that you would like to address next week? Try reflecting without judgment.

# Monday, July 13th– Sunday, July 19th

## Forecast

The Cancer vibe is at its strongest this week and the Sun, Mercury and Moon (on Saturday) are all in this intuitive, caring, creative and powerful sign. Cancer can, however, be so sensitive that it can live in the past, reviewing everything under a microscope. This is not the way to live, as it leads to sadness, regret or even depression, and so this week it's smart to brush away the cobwebs, forget what could have been and accept what is. Forgive yourself for your mistakes and forgive those you perceive to have wronged you. You have no idea what your karmic connection to them is and what lessons you are starred to learn; blame is a loser's game and being a winner is having the ability to live in the moment and create the kind of life that you wish for.

This week it's all about hearing your inner voice and training your intuition. In clearing your energy and managing it better you are in a better position to hear that voice, and to recognize the magic that is found in simple pleasures and blessings. Intuition is subtle; it needs to be trained, and to do this, it's important to stop doing anything else. Take some deep breaths and unplug from any external noise and distractions. Sit still, steady your mind and make space for your intuition. Clear your energy all week and protect it.

## Mission

- Ten minutes of meditation along with a little energy clearing and management:
    - Sit quietly, cross-legged on the floor, in the same place each day.

- ○ Inhale through your nose. Hold your breath for a few seconds and expand your tummy.
- ○ Exhale and release.
- ○ Repeat for ten minutes at least.
- At least once this week cleanse your energy with the following ritual:
  - ○ Take a bath with Epsom salts or make a scrub for the shower.
  - ○ Keep the plug in and visualize all the hurt from the past leaving your body and dropping into the water.
  - ○ Scrub your body gently, erasing the stagnant energy.
  - ○ Take the plug out and visualize the suction removing bad karma and pain along with the water. Thank the Divine Mother for absorbing this for you.
  - ○ Jump out and massage your body with some natural organic enviro-friendly body oil.

*Aspiration/mantra:* **I cleanse the past and embrace the present.**

## Monday, July 13th

The Moon moves into Taurus.
Power surge for those with stamps in Taurus and Capricorn.

**Mission completed?** Challenge level: 1–5: Ideas and insights:

_____

_____

## Tuesday, July 14th

**Mission completed?** Challenge level: 1–5: Ideas and insights:

---

---

## Wednesday, July 15th

**Mission completed?** Challenge level: 1–5: Ideas and insights:

---

---

## Thursday, July 16th

The Moon moves into Gemini. This is a good day to speak less, to listen more and to really try to hear the subtle messages of the universe that are often delivered via Earthly angels.
Power surge for those with stamps in Gemini and Capricorn.

**Mission completed?** Challenge level: 1–5: Ideas and insights:

---

---

## Friday, July 17th

Power surge for those with stamps in Pisces and Cancer.

**Mission completed?** Challenge level: 1–5: Ideas and insights:

---

---

## Saturday, July 18th

The Moon moves into Cancer.
Triply sensitive stamps today, as the Sun, Mercury and Moon are all in the sign of Cancer, which can empower us to tune in to warm feelings of love! Or cause us to overreact a little if we feel that our needs are not being met. So, chill, give others the benefit of the doubt and resolve to be happy no matter what comes your way.
Power surge for those with stamps in Cancer.

**Mission completed?** Challenge level: 1-5: Ideas and insights:

_____

_____

## Sunday, July 19th

**Mission completed?** Challenge level: 1-5: Ideas and insights:

_____

_____

# Reflections ...

If you managed to complete this week's mission, how did it make you feel?

_____

_____

If you skipped anything, did you feel any different?

_____

_____

Did you manage to complete the cleansing ritual? If so, how did it make you feel?

How did the week's aspiration unfold?

Did you notice the Cancer surge over the weekend?

List a few things, or even just one, that you are grateful for.

Are there any takeaways from this week that you would like to address next week? Try reflecting without judgment.

# Monday, July 20th– Sunday, July 26th

## Forecast

The Sun shines on Leo this week, which is rather fantabulous. Leo projects strength and a general vibe of heart and generosity ("gone right," of course) and we will have the energy to step outside our internal musings and present our ideas to the world. If you have anything you wish to say or offer to your family, friends or colleagues, this is the week to do it.

We begin the week with a New Moon in Cancer, before the Moon shifts sign to Leo. This New Moon is a great time for setting emotional intentions. You might want to lighten up and not take everything too seriously, and perhaps request a boost to your overall well-being and to the loving kindness in your life, for the good of all sentient beings. You can be both strong and loving; these traits combined are extremely powerful but seem to dissipate if our emotions are left unbridled or laced in anger and bitterness. It takes courage to forgive and bravery to love with an open heart.

The Sun moves into Leo on Wednesday, which is a huge change in energy for us all, but especially for those with major stamps in Leo. It's strong yet fun, and this week is a brilliant one for entertaining and giving your heart in all that you do.

## Mission

Whatever energy we put into the world is what we get back. This is a law of the universe and is totally incorruptible and unwavering. Some call it karma. So, your kindness will come back to you; it just may not be in the time frame that you had in mind. Don't worry about that – just be kind for the instant feel-good feeling that you get!

- Meditate daily for ten minutes.

- Do something small each day that takes you out of your comfort zone.

- Research some Yoga moves that release stale emotional energy and do them each morning, or try the following:

  ○ Assume a "tabletop" position on all fours, shoulders aligned with palms, and use your hands to push into a mat (or the floor, if you don't have a mat).

  ○ Hold your head up, take deep breaths and use your (core) tummy to power your moves and to hold you steady.

  ○ Lift your right knee out to the side at a right angle and flex your foot.

  ○ Slowly rotate your knee forward as if drawing circles; use your core to power you and don't strain your back!

  ○ Take deep breaths and visualize releasing stale emotions.

  ○ Repeat the movement rotating your knee in the opposite direction.

  ○ Repeat on both sides.

  ○ Stand up and give yourself a body shake starting at your feet!

*Aspiration/mantra:* **Courage.**

# Monday, July 20th

**New Moon in Cancer (12:33 AM EDT)**

Partial lunar eclipse. It's ritual time!

- Write down all that you wish to bring into your life this month and beyond. Focus on what you will need to boost your emotional well-being. Contemplate already having all that you desire.

- Then burn the list, asking the Divine Mother to assist you in bringing all you wish into your life.

The Moon moves into Leo.
Power surge for those with stamps in Leo and Capricorn.

**Mission completed?** Challenge level: 1–5: Ideas and insights:

# Tuesday, July 21st

**Mission completed?** Challenge level: 1–5: Ideas and insights:

## Wednesday, July 22nd

The Sun moves into Leo.
Power surge for those with stamps in Leo, Cancer and Virgo.

**Mission completed?** Challenge level: 1–5: Ideas and insights:

---

## Thursday, July 23rd

The Moon moves into Virgo. Try to get your affairs in order today; organize as much as you can and clear up any paperwork or respond to any overdue emails.

**Mission completed?** Challenge level: 1–5: Ideas and insights:

---

## Friday, July 24th

Power surge for those with stamps in Capricorn and Leo.

**Mission completed?** Challenge level: 1–5: Ideas and insights:

## Saturday, July 25th

The Moon moves into Libra.

**Mission completed?** Challenge level: 1–5: Ideas and insights:

_____

_____

## Sunday, 26th July

**Mission completed?** Challenge level: 1–5: Ideas and insights:

_____

_____

# Reflections ...

If you managed to complete this week's mission, how did it make you feel?

_____

_____

If you skipped anything, did you feel any different?

_____

_____

How did the week's aspiration unfold?

_____

_____

How was the New Moon? Did you write a manifestation list? How did it feel to actually focus on what you need emotionally?

_____

_____

Did you notice the energy shift when the Sun moved into Leo?

_____

_____

List a few things, or even just one, that you are grateful for.

_____

_____

Are there any takeaways from this week that you would like to address next week? Try reflecting without judgment.

_____

_____

# Monday, July 27th–
# Friday, July 31st

## Forecast

We start the week with the Moon in Scorpio. It's an intense and brooding sign that gives us the ability to penetrate through any veil and see what lies behind it. Truth may come to light, or deeper truths may be revealed, and we may wake up and feel completely different about certain situations.

We must be mindful not to take things too personally, though, or become defensive. Many issues can be resolved with openness and honesty and, above all else, heart. The only reason why Cancer is often deemed explosive is because it's been internalizing issues over a period of time and then someone or something innocently (well, mostly!) pushes on the wound and all hell breaks loose. But we often miss out on opportunities for growth and deep interactions by jumping the gun and reacting too quickly, due to the residual memory of past wounds. During Cancer season this tendency is intensified and so we must try to master it. Imagine playing a game of tennis with your interactions; when someone says something to you that you feel is offensive or belittling, before internalizing it and obsessing for hours, wasting precious time in second-guessing, tap the tennis ball back and ask what they meant. Do it gently and give them the opportunity to explain.

Remember, Mercury is the mischief maker! And Mercury in Cancer will have some fun in that respect. Mars in Aries is also explosive when triggered, so we must be careful this week to tread lightly, chill and keep a sense of peace within.

# Mission

Meditation is key to our life and also to our spiritual growth. This is the reason why I suggest it every day. If you skip out on any meditation practice, when you notice the difference you will at least be able to make an educated choice about what is best for you.

- This week meditate every morning for at least ten minutes before you start your day. Choose the same spot and, if you haven't already, invest in a good meditation cushion. Try to source one from a monastery or another authentic outlet, as most of them have been ethically made and also have good vibes from all of the prayers surrounding them.

- Write a note saying: "What do you mean by that?" and use it as your background on your phone or any other device that you use daily.

*Aspiration/mantra:* **I am on good terms with all. I surrender myself to none.**

## Monday, July 27th

The Moon moves into Scorpio.
Power surge for those with stamps in Scorpio and Capricorn.

**Mission completed?** Challenge level: 1–5: Ideas and insights:

## Tuesday, July 28th

**Mission completed?** Challenge level: 1–5: Ideas and insights:

_____

_____

## Wednesday, July 29th

The Moon moves into Sagittarius.
Power surge for those with stamps in Sagittarius and Capricorn.

**Mission completed?** Challenge level: 1–5: Ideas and insights:

_____

_____

## Thursday, July 30th

**Mission completed?** Challenge level: 1–5: Ideas and insights:

_____

_____

## Friday, July 31st

The Moon moves into Capricorn.
Power surge for those with stamps in Cancer and Capricorn.

**Mission completed?** Challenge level: 1–5: Ideas and insights:

_____

_____

# Reflections ...

How did the week's aspiration unfold?

_____

_____

Did you manage to play tennis with your interactions?

_____

_____

List a few things, or even just one, that you are grateful for.

_____

_____

Are there any takeaways from this week that you would like to address next week? Try reflecting without judgment.

_____

_____

Take a few moments to reflect on this month's blessings before moving on to August.

_____

_____

# August

❋

elcome to Leo season, perhaps the happiest season of them all, and with good reason! There is less rain in the northern hemisphere in August, and more sunshine, which naturally increases our vitamin D levels and boosts serotonin. A lack of sunshine affects most of us, and especially those with major Leo stamps in their chart. These lions and lionesses like to chill in the Sun, playing with their cubs or toying with their prey.

In fact Leo is lovingly known as the laziest sign in the zodiac. In the US, August 10th is National Lazy Day. Nobody knows who started it, maybe because they were too lazy to bother laying claim to it! The official day for relaxation is the 15th. This actually began in Britain, where it's known as National Slacker Day.

"August" was the name given to the month by the Roman Senate in order to honor their Emperor Augustus. It is very befitting of the regal Leo to have a month named after him.

The word "august" is also an adjective describing something, or someone, as "impressive; supreme; dignified; majestic." This fits, too, as Leo is the "king of the jungle," the strongest, most fearsome cat in town and as proud as a peacock. Leo season is all about love, courage and heart. And nothing beats heart.

Martin Luther King Jr., the father of the US civil rights movement, gave his famous "I Have a Dream" speech in this season, on August 28, 1963, combining the power of heartfelt communications with a vision.

Also, the international aid charity the Red Cross was founded on August 22, 1864, in Geneva, Switzerland.

August is a powerful month just brimming with waves of heart and compassion, and we may dial into this vibe if we wish. We all need love in our life, and in order to attract it, we have to begin to understand the concept of unconditional love. This is harder than it sounds.

## Signs in the Spotlight

 *Leo* (also its opposite sign, *Aquarius*, to a lesser degree, until the Full Moon in Aquarius on August 3rd).

 *Cancer* (also its opposite sign, *Capricorn*, to a lesser degree).

 *Gemini* (also its opposite sign, *Sagittarius*, to a lesser degree).

 *Virgo* (also its opposite sign, *Pisces*, to a lesser degree).

## Look Out for the Perseid Shower

This season is perhaps the one with the greatest potential for fun and it is often seen as the most enjoyable. The stars literally come out to play with us mere mortals as the Perseid meteor shower reaches its peak of activity on August 13th. Around this time you may catch a flash of shooting stars, triggered by the Earth passing through streams of cosmic debris left behind by asteroids and comets. If you are blessed enough to see some shooting stars, remember how fleeting life really is and perhaps instead of wishing for more, be grateful for all you have, for who you are and, most of all, for life itself.

# Opening our Heart

We begin the month with the Sun in Leo, shining in its home sign and offering us the potential to draw from its strength, create for the love of it and open our heart with courage. To live with an open heart is indeed brave but there really is no better way to embrace life.

Mercury moves into Leo on August 5th, but it won't stay long, so use this time to have fun, be playful and bask in the sunshine.

August is also the month of music and art festivals, especially in the UK, including Edinburgh's Festival Fringe (the world's largest single arts festival); Burning Man is held in the Nevada desert; Sziget happens in Budapest, Hungary; and Dimensions is held in Croatia.

This month is one for partying and having fun, for sure, and the best parties are all about the music and the atmosphere, as opposed to the clothes that you wear and the selfies you post. A real party is about enjoying the moment, not choosing a filter through which to share it with the world.

# Seeking Love

Leo season is also one in which many seek love. Folks with major stamps in Leo often need to feel recognized, adored and loved at this time. Indeed, this may be their downfall, for real love can only come from within. That's deep self-love. Note: Narcissism is not the same as self-love or self-care! This unbridled need can drive us to attract all of the opposite traits and lead to disenchantment. If what we actually seek externally is something that is missing inside us, what we gain will only last a season, if that.

Some believe that feminine energy uses sex to find love and masculine energy uses love to get sex. That's something to ponder!

# Venus: Goddess of Love, Money and Beauty

If Venus hits one of your major stamps, you are usually going to experience a short period where finances increase and your power of attraction escalates, or you may simply enjoy the pleasurable side of life, or all of the above may apply!

Venus is not known for depth and can be a tad superficial, but when the planet joins up with Cancer on August 7th, the union will bring a whole heap of kindness and care to the collective fore.

Venus remains in Cancer until next month, and it's prime time to be among people you love and to spend precious time on projects that inspire and evoke your creativity.

# Sunshine, Sex and Love

Being in the sunshine causes our melatonin levels to drop, and melatonin can block libido, so when the Sun returns so does the libido. Sex takes plenty of energy, and when people abstain, they channel that energy elsewhere. The chaste direct it toward their mind and spiritual practice, and professional athletes, ballers in particular, are often encouraged to abstain in order to conserve vital energy for a game.

Love and sex are not mutually inclusive; certainly, the former following the latter isn't a given. If you are clear about what you are seeking, this is fine, but using sex to find love rarely ends well and certainly will not attract a deep and meaningful union. For now, let's stick to love.

# Mercury Joins the Sun in Leo

Mercury moves into Leo this month, and this is a brilliant combination, especially as it connects with the Sun, too. This alignment encourages us to be happy, to cultivate gratitude and to develop our own contentment by adding to the happiness of others. Mercury influences the mind both collectively and individually, enhancing our ability to heighten our awareness and our perceptive prowess. In general, we should try to be in the moment more and care less about how we are perceived. What your own soul thinks is the key to contentment, along with your mind, body and spirit's alignment, not what others think.

Leo "gone right" is entertaining, playful and as quick to laugh at themselves as with others. Laughing at others, unless it's actual comedy, is cruel and not really a trait belonging to Leo as a time or sign.

On the flip side, and of course there is always one, Leo as a sign and season can make us ego-led, selfish and self-obsessed, and this is no longer acceptable in our Aquarian Age of enlightenment. Such behavior is seriously out of sync with the universe and will only ever attract fake, plastic situations and sycophantic people, neither of which will offer lasting soul contentment or align us with our true tribe. Remember that Leo season is all about heart, exploring what is inside our own and making it sing, giving it to projects and people, generously and without expectation. Generosity sits at the seat of the soul.

*Leo's mantra:* **I live and love with courage.**

# Saturday, August 1st– Sunday, August 2nd

## Forecast

The Sun in Leo gives our vitality and overall energy a great boost and also highlights the need to have fun. However, this weekend begins with the Moon in the uncompromising sign of Capricorn, which frowns on frivolity and can be way too serious. Combining the desire to be entertained with other practicalities will ensure that you tick all the astrology boxes.

## Mission

- Meditate each morning this weekend for ten or fifteen minutes.
- Do some exercise: venture outside (leave your phone at home), take a walk, ride a bike, go for a jog or maybe complete a few Yoga moves to open the heart and boost serotonin.
- Surround yourself with children or people with innocent playful natures.

*Aspiration/mantra:* **Playfulness.**

## Saturday, August 1st

The Moon is in Capricorn.
Daily meditation will please the discerning vibe emphasized by the Capricorn Moon and allow you to dial into Leo's playfulness when that mission is accomplished.

**Mission completed?** Challenge level: 1–5: Ideas and insights:

## Sunday, August 2nd

The Moon moves into Aquarius. This is a perfect moment to review your contribution to society, sign up to mentor someone who could benefit from your skills, or set up a direct debit to help a children's charity.
Power surge for those with stamps in Aquarius and Capricorn.

**Mission completed?** Challenge level: 1–5: Ideas and insights:

# Reflections ...

How did the weekend's aspiration unfold?

Did you manage to complete your daily meditation?

Did you exercise?

List a few things, or even just one, that you are grateful for.

Are there any takeaways from this week that you would like to address next week? Try reflecting without judgment.

# Monday, August 3rd–
# Sunday, August 9th

## Forecast

This week starts with a Full Moon in Aquarius, indicating a revolution for us and a time to leave behind anything that fails to deliver heart on some level. Release all superficial relationships and false friendships. Aquarius and Leo are in the same boat in that they value friendships and loyalty above most other things. Review your own loyalties and social circles and gently let go of anyone who doesn't have your best interests at heart. In return, review how you are as a friend and, if you find that you fall short, vow to do a better job. Loyalty is a major theme this week. If you cannot be loyal, at least be brave enough to be honest about it. If you lack loyalty in your life, look into your heart and you'll be offered real ways to change this.

## Mission

- Meditate in the same spot every morning. Ask your partner or children to join you, if you have them.

- Do one kind thing a day for a different friend. Try to do so without them knowing, if possible.

- Resolve any disputes between friends if you can and, if offered the opportunity, bring people together.

*Aspiration/mantra:* **I attract loyalty.**

## Monday, August 3rd

**Full Moon in Aquarius (11:59 AM EDT)**

Ritual time!

- Review any friendships in your life that are lacking in substance or loyalty.
- Write down the ones that you wish to release, burn the list and release your intentions to the universe.

**Mission completed?** Challenge level: 1–5: Ideas and insights:

## Tuesday, August 4th

Power surge for those with stamps in Gemini and Pisces.

**Mission completed?** Challenge level: 1–5: Ideas and insights:

## Wednesday, August 5th

The Moon moves into Pisces.
Mercury moves into Leo. This is a lighter vibe and good for humor and heart connections. Make the most of this week and pump heart into all you do. If you have no expectation of a return, you will not feel drained; on the contrary, it will energize you.

**Mission completed?** Challenge level: 1–5: Ideas and insights:

## Thursday, August 6th

**Mission completed?** Challenge level: 1–5: Ideas and insights:

## Friday, August 7th

The Moon moves into Aries.
Venus moves into Cancer. This brings a more considerate vibe to our interactions and a desire for gentle and more intimate connections.
Power surge for those with stamps in Cancer and Aries.

**Mission completed?** Challenge level: 1–5: Ideas and insights:

## Saturday, August 8th

Watch out, as the Moon and Mars are both in Aries, which is fabulous for action and passion but also has potential for anger and explosions. Stay calm and push anyone with Aries stamps to go for a run or do something to burn off that fire, so that they don't scorch those bridges or send other people running to the hills.

**Mission completed?** Challenge level: 1–5: Ideas and insights:

## Sunday, August 9th

Power surge for those with stamps in Taurus and Capricorn.

**Mission completed?** Challenge level: 1–5: Ideas and insights:

_____

_____

# Reflections ...

How did the week's aspiration unfold?

_____

_____

Did you complete a Full Moon ritual? If so, what did you release?

_____

_____

Did you feel the Aries/fire boost on Saturday and Sunday?

_____

_____

List a few things, or even just one, that you are grateful for.

_____

_____

Are there any takeaways from this week that you would like to address next week? Try reflecting without judgment.

# Monday, August 10th– Sunday, August 16th

## Forecast

The week starts with the Moon in Taurus, and that, combined with the Sun and Mercury in Leo, may direct us to spend some time on self-nourishment or even on our appearance or other areas or activities that boost our confidence and feel-good factor. Leo is all about the hair (the mane) and Taurus values the finest food and goodies in general, as well as sensuality. So, do something nice for yourself, and your partner, if you have one. Cook some nourishing food and take time out to feel good on every level.

## Mission

- Meditate each morning, alone or with your family.

- Try sitting under a tree, allowing yourself to connect to its solid strength and roots.

- Book a blow dry, or new hairstyle, at a salon for yourself or your partner. Or book a massage, or give your partner one, with candles and essential oils to evoke sensual pleasure.

- Cook some lovely healthy food on Sunday and invite friends and family to join you to eat it. Find recipes, if you need to, and cook from scratch.

*Aspiration/mantra:* **Sensuality.**

## Monday, August 10th

**National Lazy Day.**
The Moon moves into Taurus.

**Mission completed?** Challenge level: 1–5: Ideas and insights:

## Tuesday, August 11th

**Mission completed?** Challenge level: 1–5: Ideas and insights:

## Wednesday, August 12th

The Moon moves into Gemini.
Power surge for those with stamps in Gemini and Capricorn.

**Mission completed?** Challenge level: 1–5: Ideas and insights:

## Thursday, August 13th

**Mission completed?** Challenge level: 1–5: Ideas and insights:

## Friday, August 14th

Power surge for those with stamps in Aries and Cancer.

**Mission completed?** Challenge level: 1–5: Ideas and insights:

---

## Saturday, August 15th

**National Relaxation Day.**
The Moon moves into Cancer.
Uranus goes retrograde in Taurus. Uranus hasn't retrograded since the first two weeks in January: this phase is now asking you to revisit any good intentions that you made back then and to review how they are coming along. Any seeds planted then will need some attention now. Our values are also tested under this phase, and it's a good time to check in with your higher mind in order to hear the subtle directions from your soul. Uranus is known as "the great awakener," so some deeper truths may come to light, giving you a wake-up call.

**Mission completed?** Challenge level: 1–5: Ideas and insights:

---

## Sunday, August 16th

The Moon and Venus connect in Cancer, which makes it a wonderful time for giving your time and energy to family and loved ones. Create a nurturing space, buy a board game and convince everyone to ditch their phones during the game. Power surge for those with stamps in Leo and Capricorn.

**Mission completed?** Challenge level: 1–5: Ideas and insights:

_____

_____

# Reflections ...

How did the week's aspiration unfold?

_____

_____

Did you dial in to the sensual vibe?

_____

_____

Did you feel the homey, sensitive Cancer vibe on Sunday?

_____

_____

List a few things, or even just one, that you are grateful for.

_____

_____

Are there any takeaways from this week that you would like to address next week? Try reflecting without judgment.

_____

_____

# Monday, August 17th– Sunday, August 23rd

## Forecast

This week begins with the Sun and Moon in Leo. This is wonderful, as the masculine and feminine energies in us all, and collectively, are equalized. These are the last few days of the Sun in Leo, and if you have major stamps in the sign, make hay while the Sun shines upon you. Be free, dance as if nobody is watching you and embrace your childlike nature, the one enchanted by the magic of the universe and delighted by the fact that you are alive.

Whatever your major stamps, prepare for the New Moon in Leo by thinking about what you need to attract to be happier, or, if you are already content, how you can assist in the happiness of others. The New Moon is an incredibly powerful phase – a time when karma is magnified and we have the ability to manifest. So, try your best to banish worry, anxiety and negative thoughts from your life, be positive and focus on sunshine and joy, and do good things for others, without expectations.

## Mission

- Meditate daily for at least ten minutes.
- Play music while you are getting dressed. Music has power and sometimes people forget the impact it has on mood. If you know what music brings you joy, then hit "play"; if you need some inspiration, do a little search to find a playlist, or book a ticket to see live music events or sing and dance.

*Aspiration/mantra:* **Joy**.

## Monday, August 17th

The Moon moves into Leo.

**Mission completed?** Challenge level: 1–5: Ideas and insights:

---

## Tuesday, August 18th

### New Moon in Leo (10:42 PM EDT)

This is a powerful time to focus on your heart's desires and draw closer to what, and who, you love.

- Light some candles, set the scene and invite your partner, family or friends to join you. It's a good exercise for adults and children alike to think about what you want and what you believe will make you happy.

- Write all your desires down on paper, sit for a few moments contemplating them in silence and cultivate gratitude by thanking the universe for all the wonderful people and things that you already have in your life.

- Then burn the paper.

**Mission completed?** Challenge level: 1–5: Ideas and insights:

---

# Wednesday, August 19th

The Moon moves into Virgo.
Power surge for those with stamps in Leo and Virgo.

**Mission completed?** Challenge level: 1–5: Ideas and insights:

---

# Thursday, August 20th

Mercury moves into Virgo. This impacts our mind, both collectively and personally, resulting in the need for detail. Avoid being overly critical or controlling; do as much as you can and then let go and live a little. If others are channeling this behavior, it's due to fear. So, be patient and kind.

**Mission completed?** Challenge level: 1–5: Ideas and insights:

---

# Friday, August 21st

The Moon moves into Libra.
Power surge for those with stamps in Libra and Capricorn.

**Mission completed?** Challenge level: 1–5: Ideas and insights:

## Saturday, August 22nd

The Sun moves into Virgo. This is a major shift in energy and while it's amazing for those with stamps in Virgo, the rest of us have to decrease our potential for stress and anxieties triggered by over-the-top and unrealistic expectations.

**Mission completed?** Challenge level: 1–5: Ideas and insights:

_____

_____

## Sunday, August 23rd

Power surge for those with stamps in Scorpio and Capricorn.

**Mission completed?** Challenge level: 1–5: Ideas and insights:

_____

_____

# Reflections ...

How did the week's aspiration unfold?

_____

_____

Did you notice an increase in joy in your daily routine?

_____

_____

Did you feel the energy shift when the Sun and Mercury switched signs into Virgo?

How was the New Moon ritual?

List a few things, or even just one, that you are grateful for.

Are there any takeaways from this week that you would like to address next week? Try reflecting without judgment.

# Monday, August 24th– Monday, August 31st

## Forecast

The Sun is now in Virgo, along with Mercury, which automatically pushes the "logic" button. There is the tendency to overanalyze or be too self-critical when Virgo is in the spotlight, as we expect nothing short of perfection, but the only thing that is ever perfect is the moment we are in. The future isn't promised to any of us and the most important thing we can do is to be in the here and now.

Virgo often causes past-life issues to be dragged up with no explanation, and this needs to be managed. If it happens, flood yourself with feel-good juices, know that you are safe and do something that lightens your mood, reduces anxiety and destresses you. Meditation is key to balancing the energy this week and will enable you to tune in to the higher vibration of Virgo, which is all about faith, trust and purity of heart.

## Mission

- Fifteen minutes of meditation each morning ... before you even consider looking at your phone!

- Deep breaths during the day: three in a row without interruption.

- Book tickets for a comedy club. Go with your partner, friends, or even alone. It doesn't matter who you're with; what matters is that you go and laugh. Nothing heals like laughter.

*Aspiration/mantra:* **This very moment is perfect.**

## Monday, August 24th

**Mission completed?** Challenge level: 1–5: Ideas and insights:

_____

_____

## Tuesday, August 25th

The Moon moves into Sagittarius.
Power surge for those with stamps in Sagittarius and Capricorn.

**Mission completed?** Challenge level: 1–5: Ideas and insights:

_____

_____

## Wednesday, August 26th

**Mission completed?** Challenge level: 1–5: Ideas and insights:

_____

_____

## Thursday, August 27th

The Moon moves into Capricorn.
Power surge for those with stamps in Aries and Cancer.

**Mission completed?** Challenge level: 1–5: Ideas and insights:

_____

_____

# Friday, August 28th

**Mission completed?** Challenge level: 1–5: Ideas and insights:

_____

_____

# Saturday, August 29th

Power surge for those with stamps in Aries and Aquarius.

**Mission completed?** Challenge level: 1–5: Ideas and insights:

_____

_____

# Sunday, August 30th

The Moon moves into Aquarius.

**Mission completed?** Challenge level: 1–5: Ideas and insights:

_____

_____

# Monday, August 31st

**Mission completed?** Challenge level: 1–5: Ideas and insights:

_____

_____

Before you flick the page and jump into September, take a moment to review August and enjoy the last day of the month.

# Reflections ...

How did the week's aspiration unfold?

_____

_____

Did you notice the Virgo drive to attain perfection?

_____

_____

Did you book tickets to a comedy club?

_____

_____

List a few things, or even just one, that you are grateful for.

_____

_____

Are there any takeaways from this week that you would like to address next week? Try reflecting without judgment.

_____

_____

Take a few moments to appreciate all that you've accomplished this month before you move on to September.

_____

_____

# September

⚛

**W**elcome to September, also known as Virgo season. Virgo and its opposite sign, Pisces, are the coolest cats (or fish!) in town. "September" derives from the Latin word for "seven," *septem*, as it was the seventh month of the year in the old Roman calendar.

Britain switched to the Gregorian calendar we all use today in September 1752, after much analysis. A trait very much owned by Virgo.

## Signs in the Spotlight

 *Virgo* (also its opposite sign, *Pisces*, to a lesser degree, until the Full Moon in Pisces on September 9th).

 *Libra* (also its opposite sign, *Aries*, equally).

 *Cancer* (also its opposite sign, *Capricorn*, equally).

 *Leo* (also its opposite sign, Aquarius, to a lesser degree).

# The Search for Perfection

We begin the month with the Sun shining in the sign of Virgo, along with Mercury, and it's also the start of a new academic year and back to work for many of us. Virgo as a sign and time is all about sharpening focus and expanding the mind with wisdom and academic pursuits: it needs organization, analysis, control and order to achieve its potential, although we must examine our expectations and ensure that we are not treading a barren path on a fruitless search for perfection. It usually takes a long time to realize that the only thing that can ever be deemed perfect is the very moment that we are in right now.

Virgo "gone right" is focused on service to others. I actually heard someone say once that charity begins at home and so I explained that every spiritual master says the same thing: we are all connected by our collective energy and when any one of us suffers, we all do. Also, it's a scientifically proven fact that helping others increases our own feelings of usefulness and happiness. So, it makes sense that when we can, and certainly if we have the luxury of time and money, we should help people who are less fortunate. This increases our karmic merit, and trust me, this is the only credit you really need in the bank. Money doesn't make the world go round, karma does!

# Back to School

Stress, anxiety and worry levels are at an all-time high during Virgo season. I used to think this was just because I had to return to school or work after a lovely long vacation, but now I know it's the season's natural greeting! Therefore, we need to do all that we can to reduce the potential for stress and protect our fragile mind. When we have tools that all do their jobs successfully, we may then help others to use them too. For those with major stamps in the sign of Virgo, the above is even more essential.

Virgo season is a prime time to learn and to polish our knowledge; Virgo is a smart sign which encourages a desire for hard evidence and facts over fiction. It is also a practical sign that pushes us to face our vulnerabilities and work on them.

Work – it's all about work this month, either business pursuits or self-improvement, or perhaps both.

# Slow Down, Take Stock

Mars is still in its home sign, Aries, although it switches its energy output and retrogrades on the 9th, staying that way until November. This gives us the opportunity to slow down and assess the path we are on, reviewing it objectively without any rose-tinted glasses and making any changes we need to improve our overall health and well-being.

Pluto in Capricorn is retrograde until next month, which is good news, as it gives us all a little break from the Capricorn rule!

Neptune in Pisces is also retrograde until next month, and that one can go either way: "gone wrong" means fear, lack of clarity and more anxiety; "gone right" means revising our dreams, tuning in to our imagination and hearing our spiritual voice amid the noise and haste. The choice is ours.

# Improving Overall Health and Well-being

Every sign governs an industry, and the health and healing industry is governed by Virgo. Many folks with major stamps in Virgo would scoff at the credibility of astrology full stop, but Hippocrates, known as the "Father of Medicine," said: "A physician with no knowledge of astrology has no right to call himself a physician." At the time, both astrologers and astronomers were respected academic figures and we shouldn't forget this.

A good example of the importance of astrology in healing is Nicholas Culpeper's *Complete Herbal*, which matches ailments and herbs with planets, signs and times. Culpeper was an English botanist, physician and astrologer whose book was first published in 1653, but more recent research still indicates that herbal remedies are the way forward in some cases, especially in managing anxiety and stress.

Talking of which, this month is Suicide Prevention Awareness Month. The issue of suicide is real, and we must play our part by caring for other people, talking and actually listening and, if we need help ourselves, we have to be brave enough to ask for it, so that we may use the current alignments of stars to heal ourselves and others.

Most sensitive and creative folks I know suffer with blue moods or days, feeling despair at the lack of humanity on our planet. Personally, I found that changing my daily routine changed my life for the better: now if I'm feeling a wave of despair coming on, I roll out my mat, meditate, and practice Yoga. Change your routine and life flows like the practice.

# Galloping Minds and Feng Shui

When our mind gallops into the future or reverses into the past it causes us nothing but problems, so a really effective remedy is training it to be present!

This month's missions are focused on stress management and service. To reduce stress, we first have to feng shui our own life. Don't worry, you don't need a joyful Japanese lady accompanied by cameras to clear your closets and life, the simple weekly missions will help you do it. Try it – it's liberating.

*Virgo's mantra:* **As I exhale, I release and surrender.**

# Tuesday, September 1st– Sunday, September 6th

## Forecast

The Sun and Mercury are both in Virgo and the energy is ripe for productivity, but strategy and planning are required. We all need to clean up our environment and our life. Our environment is a direct reflection of our mind, so make it Zen. No pressure! Begin at home, one room each day or night: turn out the cupboards and clear the clutter, recycle, donate to charity ... Even the clutter you cannot see will impact your stress levels. Sort through paperwork and be free to release it all under the Full Moon in Pisces on Wednesday and do a happy dance.

This week is well starred to help you to align with your dreams and imagination, but do prepare first. The smartest artists and creatives I know are in control of the process and always work from a clean slate in order to produce their best work. This may seem elementary, but it works. Creativity and inspiration will flow freely if the preparation is precise.

If your space is already pristine and organized, help someone else to declutter, but be patient. Emotions (particularly fear and sadness) hide behind noise and clutter, so be gentle with yourself and others throughout the process. Play happy music, open the windows, and if you're helping someone else, don't take any snipes personally. The demanding vibe of Virgo should switch when Mercury moves into the calm sign of Libra, enhancing the potential for peaceful and harmonious interactions.

## Mission

- Meditate each day and sit in silence, where possible, letting thoughts go and bringing your attention calmly back to your breath.

- It takes twenty-eight days to form a healthy habit or to break a bad one.

This month, vow to ditch the unhelpful ones and adopt new ones. Choose one to leave behind and one to take up, recording your progress in your journal each day.

- Sign up to become a volunteer for a phone-line support service. Be available to listen to a stranger who is suffering and give them your time and heart: help them to feel connected. Or make a donation.

*Aspiration/mantra:* **I find joy in service.**

## Tuesday, September 1st

The Moon moves into Pisces. Get organized and then prepare to go with the Pisces flow.
Power surge for those with stamps in Aries and Pisces.

**Mission completed?** Challenge level: 1–5: Ideas and insights:

## Wednesday, September 2nd

### Full Moon in Pisces (1:23 AM EDT)

Ritual time!

- Collect any paperwork that you have cleared and then write a list of the fears and worries that you may need to release. Then burn the whole bunch (safely).

- Note how good you feel.

224

**Mission completed?** Challenge level: 1–5: Ideas and insights:

_____

_____

# Thursday, September 3rd

The Moon moves into Aries.
Power surge for those with stamps in Cancer and Aries.

**Mission completed?** Challenge level: 1–5: Ideas and insights:

_____

_____

# Friday, September 4th

On this day, in 1781, Los Angeles was founded by forty-four Spanish settlers. It was originally called _El Pueblo de Nuestra Señora la Reina de los Ángeles_, or "The Town of Our Lady the Queen of the Angels."
The Moon and Mars connect in Aries today. Use this energy to bounce into action and tackle your space-clearing, or any other projects, with gusto!

**Mission completed?** Challenge level: 1–5: Ideas and insights:

_____

_____

## Saturday, September 5th

Mercury moves into Libra. This should dial down the collective critical energy and turn the focus toward more diplomacy and less judgment.

**Mission completed?** Challenge level: 1–5: Ideas and insights:

_____

_____

## Sunday, September 6th

The Moon moves into Taurus.
Venus moves into Leo. This is a fabulous energy and a great star combination: it evokes Leo heart for all and gives us the freedom to be playful but still tackle any issues that we may have with humour, strength and courage!
Power surge for those with stamps in Aries and Taurus.

**Mission completed?** Challenge level: 1–5: Ideas and insights:

_____

_____

# Reflections ...

How did the week's aspiration unfold?

_____

_____

Did you complete a Full Moon ritual? If so, what did you release and was the ritual helpful?

Did you manage to clear any clutter? How did it make you feel?

List a few things, or even just one, that you are grateful for.

Are there any takeaways from this week that you would like to address next week? Try reflecting without judgment.

# Monday, September 7th–Sunday, September 13th

## Forecast

Mars begins its retrograde phase, which lasts until next month, and the effects of this will be stronger than usual because it's in its home sign. Mars retrograde can cause us to face any issues by being over assertive or even angry. The latter is never helpful: when we feel angry we are out of control, and this emotion doesn't sit right with Virgo in charge. So, try to avoid confrontations, and instead assert yourself lovingly and calmly, speak your truth and know that nobody can cause you to "feel" anything; you are solely in charge of how you feel. There may be a shift in your overall energy levels, so try to find alternative methods of exercise and protect your energy. If you feel stressed, find new ways to combat this: natural remedies such as herbal supplements, teas (chamomile and lavender), exercise, meditation and healthy routines are a huge help. You can channel Aries (the sign of leadership) "gone right" by leading by example and being passionate, dynamic and action-oriented.

This week we also remember the devastating terrorist attack on the World Trade Center on September 11th. Interestingly, on the same day back in 1893, the world's first organized interfaith gathering took place in Chicago.

Anger never solves anything, and we can help to raise the collective energy by transforming those feelings into compassion for, indeed, no good, bad or ignorant deed ever goes unnoticed. This is the law of karma. Try to avoid being judgmental of either yourself or others and flick your mental switch to kindness and compassion. This is the way of the spiritual warrior.

# Mission

- Meditate every day for at least ten minutes and breathe in calming vibes.
- Assert yourself gently, without anger, aggression or passive aggression.
- Continue with your space-clearing and get organized.
- Light a candle on Friday and repeat the following mantra: "May all beings be happy and free from the causes of suffering."

*Aspiration/mantra:* **Inner calm and outer peace.**

## Monday, September 7th

**Mission completed?** Challenge level: 1–5: Ideas and insights:

_____

_____

## Tuesday, September 8th

The Moon moves into Gemini.
Power surge for those with stamps in Gemini and Capricorn.

**Mission completed?** Challenge level: 1–5: Ideas and insights:

_____

_____

## Wednesday, September 9th

Mars goes retrograde in Aries.

**Mission completed?** Challenge level: 1–5: Ideas and insights:

## Thursday, September 10th

The Moon moves into Cancer.

**Mission completed?** Challenge level: 1–5: Ideas and insights:

## Friday, September 11th

The Inauguration of the Parliament of the World's Religions took place in 1893, in Chicago. This was the world's first organized interfaith gathering and was an attempt to open up communications to promote understanding, unite all faiths and create world peace.
Power surge for those with stamps in Aries and Cancer.

**Mission completed?** Challenge level: 1–5: Ideas and insights:

## Saturday, September 12th

**Mission completed?** Challenge level: 1–5: Ideas and insights:

_____

_____

## Sunday, September 13th

The Moon moves into Leo.
Jupiter goes direct in Capricorn.
Power surge for those with stamps in Aries and Leo.

**Mission completed?** Challenge level: 1–5: Ideas and insights:

_____

_____

# Reflections ...

How did the week's aspiration unfold?

_____

_____

Did you carry out the ritual on Friday?

_____

_____

Did you encounter anger? If so, how did you handle it?

Did you manage to clear any clutter? How did it make you feel?

List a few things, or even just one, that you are grateful for.

Are there any takeaways from this week that you would like to address next week? Try reflecting without judgment.

# Monday, September 14th– Sunday, September 20th

## Forecast

The week commences with plenty of sparks and fire, both collectively and for those with stamps in Leo.

By the time we reach Tuesday, the Moon shifts into Virgo and connects with the Sun in preparation for the New Moon on Thursday. This New Moon, in Virgo, is an excellent time to undertake in a purification process and to conduct an overhaul of our habits to see if they fail to serve our higher self or, indeed, the greater good.

Overall, this week is perfect for giving back and boosting our sense of responsibility and service. You do not have to make a grand gesture, but remember that people all over are suffering: a smile or kind word to a stranger can lift spirits and being present and available to listen deeply to people will heal us all, on so many levels.

## Mission

- Meditate for at least ten minutes each day, longer if possible:
  - Focus on your breath and feel how relaxing it is to take deep breaths.
  - Inhale and push your shoulders back, as if trying to make your shoulder blades meet. Exhale and push your shoulders forward.
  - Repeat.
- Focus on clearing one room or space each day, at home or at work.

*Aspiration/mantra:* **I am in control.**

# Monday, September 14th

The Moon and Venus connect in Leo. Be sure to channel the "gone right" vibe, avoiding selfishness and drama queens or attention seekers. Give heart to all you do and keep generosity to the fore in your mind.

**Mission completed?** Challenge level: 1–5: Ideas and insights:

# Tuesday, September 15th

The Moon moves into Virgo.
Power surge for those with stamps in Aries and Virgo.

**Mission completed?** Challenge level: 1–5: Ideas and insights:

# Wednesday, September 16th

**Mexican Independence Day.**

**Mission completed?** Challenge level: 1–5: Ideas and insights:

## Thursday, September 17th

### New Moon in Virgo (6:00 AM EDT)

Ritual time!

- Write a list of the new habits you wish to bring in and say a mantra that reminds you to purify your mind through prayer and meditation; your body through deep practices, such as Yoga and *Qi Gong*, and being mindful of the sort of food you consume – avoid toxins and keep it pure – and your spirit by refusing to engage in divisive, low-vibe communications and by surrounding yourself with spiritually inclined friends.

The Moon then moves into Libra.
Power surge for those with stamps in Libra and Capricorn.

**Mission completed?** Challenge level: 1–5: Ideas and insights:

## Friday, September 18th

**Mission completed?** Challenge level: 1–5: Ideas and insights:

## Saturday, September 19th

The Moon moves into Scorpio.
Power surge for those with stamps in Aries and Scorpio.

**Mission completed?** Challenge level: 1–5: Ideas and insights:

_____

_____

## Sunday, September 20th

**Mission completed?** Challenge level: 1–5: Ideas and insights:

_____

_____

# Reflections ...

How did the week's aspiration unfold?

_____

_____

Did you carry out the New Moon ritual on Thursday?

_____

_____

Did you sign up to volunteer?

Did you do anything to purify yourself this week? If so, how did you feel?

Did you manage to clear any clutter? How did it make you feel?

List a few things, or even just one, that you are grateful for.

Are there any takeaways from this week that you would like to address next week? Try reflecting without judgment.

# Monday, September 21st–
# Sunday, September 27th

## Forecast

There is a shift in the overall vibe this week and you may choose to use that to your advantage.

When the Moon moves into Sagittarius on Tuesday, seek inspiration: you may plan an adventure or just step off your beaten track in order to find people and wisdom that will feed your higher mind and lift your spirits.

The Sun moves into Libra, and this is a major boost for those with stamps in Libra, although it can heighten our expectations of ourselves and others, so keeping a sense of perspective and acceptance is key to growing your inner contentment.

Mercury shifts into Scorpio on Sunday, which magnifies a desire for introspection. Hit the "pause" button if you find yourself playing the blame game and only venture deeply inside if it's to meditate.

Keep your serotonin levels high this weekend.

## Mission

- Meditate every day for at least ten minutes. Do not use anything other than your breath to do this: sit, breathe, repeat.

- Exercise every day to keep serotonin levels high (ten minutes at least, and yes, walking counts. Be in the moment with every step and only use your phone if it's to play good music that will make you walk faster!).

*Aspiration/mantra:* **I meet my own expectations.**

## Monday, September 21st

Power surge for those with stamps in Virgo and Sagittarius.

**Mission completed?** Challenge level: 1–5: Ideas and insights:

_____

_____

## Tuesday, September 22nd

Today we celebrate the equinox, which is when the Earth's equator passes through the center of the Sun, and day and night are of almost equal length all over the planet. In the northern hemisphere, we welcome the beginning of autumn, and as temperatures usually start to decrease, we traditionally harvest our crops and begin to store our supplies for the winter months. In the southern hemisphere, it is the beginning of spring, when we welcome green shoots and warmer days.

The Sun moves into Libra.
The Moon moves into Sagittarius.

**Mission completed?** Challenge level: 1–5: Ideas and insights:

_____

_____

## Wednesday, September 23rd

Power surge for those with stamps in Aries and Capricorn.

**Mission completed?** Challenge level: 1–5: Ideas and insights:

_____

_____

## Thursday, September 24th

The Moon moves into Capricorn.

**Mission completed?** Challenge level: 1–5: Ideas and insights:

## Friday, September 25th

**Mission completed?** Challenge level: 1–5: Ideas and insights:

## Saturday, September 26th

The Moon moves into Aquarius.
Power surge for those with stamps in Libra and Aquarius.

**Mission completed?** Challenge level: 1–5: Ideas and insights:

## Sunday, September 27th

Mercury moves into Scorpio.

**Mission completed?** Challenge level: 1–5: Ideas and insights:

# Reflections ...

How did the week's aspiration unfold?

Did you do any exercise this week? If so, how did you feel?

List a few things, or even just one, that you are grateful for.

Are there any takeaways from this week that you would like to address next week? Try reflecting without judgment.

# Monday, September 28th– Wednesday, September 30th

## Forecast

We can all have a little chill on Monday, when the Moon moves into dreamy Pisces, but be prepared, Saturn has returned from its retrograde holiday and is back in its home sign, Capricorn. "Here we go again," you may be saying, but don't stress too much, just know that Saturn makes Virgo season seem like a picnic in the park: it takes no prisoners and flags up issues that we need to tackle. It can all be a little serious, so make sure that you have your toolkit ready: exercise, keep your serotonin levels high, meditate and do all that you can to ensure that projects are on track and that you keep any promises you've made, or communicate honestly if you can't. That way you are in the clear. Mercury in Scorpio likes to dig up the past and blow cobwebs away, so just walk with your truth and be strong. Keep perspective and don't slip down the rabbit hole or try to hide from anything.

## Mission

- Meditate every day.
- Face fears or issues from the past: expose them to light so that you may move on:
  - Create a list of what you wish to achieve in your relationships and leave it there for now.
  - Spend time alone, quiet your chattering mind and let your soul speak.

*Aspiration/mantra:* **When my soul speaks, I listen.**

## Monday, September 28th

The Moon moves into Pisces.
Power surge for those with stamps in Aries and Pisces.

**Mission completed?** Challenge level: 1–5: Ideas and insights:

## Tuesday, September 29th

Saturn goes direct.

**Mission completed?** Challenge level: 1–5: Ideas and insights:

## Wednesday, September 30th

Power surge for those with stamps in Capricorn and Aries.

**Mission completed?** Challenge level: 1–5: Ideas and insights:

# Reflections ...

How did the week's aspiration unfold?

Did you notice when Saturn stepped back in?

Did you notice any fears arising? If so, what did you do?

Did you do anything to purify yourself during the past this week? If so, how did you feel?

List a few things, or even just one, that you are grateful for.

Are there any takeaways from this week that you would like to address next week? Try reflecting without judgment.

Next month is almost here, so relax before you move on to the next month. You will never get this moment back, so raise a glass, light a candle and thank the universe for walking with you ... always!

# October

Octber, or Libra season, is here. Libra, as a sign and time, is all about love and relationships. Venus, the ruler of Libra, evokes beauty, charm and peace and highlights the need for balance, among many other things. The star alignments this month encourage us to address any areas of our life that are off-balance. Due to the heavy Scorpio influence it will be challenging for us to just skim above the surface; we are better off facing issues with insight and without aggression.

## Signs in the Spotlight

*Libra* (also its opposite sign, *Aries*, to a lesser degree, until the Full Moon in Aries on October 1st).

*Scorpio* (also its opposite sign, *Taurus*, to a lesser degree).

*Sagittarius* (also its opposite sign, *Gemini*, to a lesser degree).

## Relationships and Redressing the Balance

Libra, as a sign and season, is seriously focused on relationships. Many people don't usually like to be alone at this time, and they absolutely abhor it if they have major Libra stamps in their full charts. This often leads to all sorts of issues: the inability to be alone can make people hop from one disastrous union to another, and the same wounds will keep manifesting until we face them. No person or external situation can fulfill a needy person. Neediness can also cause us to lower our standards, associating with people, or settling for partners and lovers, who do not bring out the best in us, and vice versa. We have to validate ourselves, be comfortable with our own company and cultivate calm through silence and tranquillity.

# Feed the Right Inner Wolf

Humans are a little like pack animals. We each have a gentle wolf inside us, but also a dangerous one, and it's up to us which one of them sees the most light, in terms of how much we feed them. Some of us may be lone wolves, but none of us can exist in complete solitude. Our connections to others have the potential to make us both extremely happy and extremely sad, if we allow them to. If we "need" others to complete us, we are asking for trouble. We each came onto the planet alone (albeit with a little help!), and when we leave the planet, we shall also be alone; and in between the only constant is our own soul, or mind, whichever you prefer to call it. This is why it's essential to be at peace with your soul, and you can only do that by taking the time to listen to it and nurture it.

The major lesson for Libra to learn is peace. Peace is a very Libran theme. Although the concept was formulated during the season of Capricorn (the sign that governs), the United Nations was actually formed in October 1945, with the sole aim of maintaining international peace and security. And Alfred Nobel, founder of the Nobel Peace Prize, was born on October 21st in 1883.

# Cultivating Inner Peace

Cultivating our own inner peace is perhaps the most valuable method of self-improvement on the planet and the best gift that we can give to humanity and the Divine Mother. Speaking our truth is vital to our own well-being and for strengthening our soul, but being at peace with others is perhaps of equal importance and we can do so without surrendering truth or integrity. Some people will fight for their truth, or simply to be heard, but this is neither the solution nor the way of the spiritual warrior: far better to lead by example, to be at peace with your own decisions and resist without violence. Violence is not just physical; it comes in many forms. As Mars is still in Aries (the opposite sign to Libra) this potential is magnified at this time, and Mars is retrograde, so patience will be required. This aspect could play out in several different ways, depending on how strong Aries and Libra are in your own chart, but to summarize, energy levels may be a little low and tolerance levels may not be as high as they usually are during Libra season. I will give you the heads-up on the weeks and days when this is particularly strong. If you are aware of this and can spark intelligent debate when facing difficult situations, then you have the power to awaken someone long enough for them to question their bad behavior or ignorant opinions. That is enough.

# Romance, Beauty and Rhythm

Jupiter and Saturn are now both direct in Capricorn and this combination pushes us to get serious about our commitments and to operate discerningly. We have the tools that can help us to manage our energy this month, restraint being one of them. Being out of control will not be well received by Jupiter and Saturn, who are both working with discerning Capricorn. Grace and decorum are traits commonly associated with both the goddess Venus and Libra as a sign and a time. However, both Venus and Libra can also be judgmental and loud, overly emotional or aggressive folks are often quietly judged. But bottling emotions is never a wise move, and unleashing them on others in the form of anger, impatience or resentment is seriously frowned upon by Venus and the law of karma. Good manners are simple; just remember to take other people's needs into consideration. If we all do that, everyone's needs are covered, and we can all work together in harmony ... and we keep Venus happy!

# Poetry

Because the Sun is shining in Libra, it is asking us to bring more grace and art, of any form, into our life. Libra is ruled by Venus, and this planet is all about beauty, romance, balanced unions and of course the arts.

Poetry is an intense art form that describes feelings and emotions in a rhythmic flow, and so many great musicians and lyricists, such as John Lennon, Paul Simon, Sting, Tom Petty, Snoop Dogg and Eminem (all born in this month), could also be seen as poets.

In the UK, National Poetry Day, founded in 1994 by William Sieghart, is celebrated in late September/early October. Quite a few of the country's greatest poets were born in the month of October: John Keats, for example, was born in October 1795. Tragic Keats, who was only twenty-five when he died, became a key player in the Romantic movement that shaped an artistic era. Dylan Thomas, Swansea's most famous son, was born in October 1914, and, as is the way with Libra "gone right," he was a pacifist and vehemently anti-fascist, holding close links to communist groups.

*Libra's mantra:* **I validate myself.**

# Thursday, October 1st– Sunday, October 4th

## Forecast

This week, it's important to assess and address our own needs and re-evaluate our relationships, including the one we have with ourselves. If our partnerships are not balanced, then they are likely to cause more problems than we may have anticipated when we agreed to form them. In order to function properly, we need positive relationships. So, be brave and let go of those that you have for purely superficial reasons or just to fend off loneliness, but let go without burning any bridges, as this will allow you to make room for your true tribe while giving friends and lovers the opportunity to grow and then, perhaps, return.

Libra season is brimming with opportunities to form new unions and dissolve agreements that we may have outgrown or those which no longer serve our higher purpose.

The Full Moon in Aries, on Thursday, is a perfect time to release anything that is unbalanced. Complete the ritual and begin the month with a fresh mind and clean slate.

## Mission

- Meditate every day, for at least ten minutes.
- Stop feeding narcissistic behavior: try not to take, post or "like" any selfies.
- Appreciate the natural beauty found in character and nature.

*Aspiration/mantra:* **My relationships are balanced and real.**

## Thursday, October 1st

### Full Moon in Aries (5:06 PM EDT)

Ritual time!

- Write a list of anything, or anyone, negative that sparks your anger.
- List the areas in your life that are not balanced.
- Burn the list and feel the release.

The Moon moves into Aries.

**Mission completed?** Challenge level: 1–5: Ideas and insights:

## Friday, October 2nd

Venus moves into Virgo. Watch out for high expectations and the need for perfection; avoid spending too much time pursuing love or adoration from anyone; tune in to your soul and be happy in the moment. Let it all come to you just by being yourself.

**Mission completed?** Challenge level: 1–5: Ideas and insights:

## Saturday, October 3rd

The Moon moves into Taurus.
Power surge for those with stamps in Capricorn and Taurus.

**Mission completed?** Challenge level: 1–5: Ideas and insights:

## Sunday, October 4th

Pluto goes direct in Capricorn.

**Mission completed?** Challenge level: 1–5: Ideas and insights:

# Reflections ...

How did the week's aspiration unfold?

Did you manage to complete your daily meditation?

How easy were the other parts of the mission?

How was the Full Moon ritual?

List a few things, or even just one, that you are grateful for.

Are there any takeaways from this week that you would like to address next week? Try reflecting without judgment.

# Monday, October 5th– Sunday, October 11th

## Forecast

This is likely to be an intense week: one where superficiality just won't cut it. With Venus flowing in Virgo, we are asked to purify our hearts and unions.

Mercury is in Scorpio, which results in deep and penetrating thoughts and the potential for thought-provoking revelations and communications. Obviously, this can go wrong, too, leading to criticism or obsession. Flip the latter, in yourself, by taking a moment to change your energy and, if you are on the receiving end, examine the motivation behind the behavior and respond accordingly. Facing our insecurities can help us to grow in ways we never dreamed possible. Ask for help if you need to but discern who has the potential to assist you before oversharing.

Purification is also wise this week: clear your environment first, especially if you work in the creative industries, but, even if you don't, you will still find it liberating to allow some fresh clean energy into your life.

## Mission

- Meditate every day for at least ten minutes:
    - While still sitting cross-legged, stretch your arms out wide, palms facing upward.
    - Inhale and bring your hands to the tips of your shoulders. Exhale and roll your elbows forward, as if drawing circles in the air.
    - Repeat slowly. You will be likely to hear, and feel, a few clicks. This is good: it's a release of stagnant *dukka*.

○     Repeat the practice the other way.

● Feng shui your phone and email. Clear the spam, unsubscribe, delete all negative communications that you no longer need and clear your trash. Delete or block contacts that you want, or need, to leave behind.

## Monday, October 5th

Power surge for those with stamps in Capricorn and Gemini.

**Mission completed?** Challenge level: 1–5: Ideas and insights:

---

## Tuesday, October 6th

The Moon moves into Gemini.

**Mission completed?** Challenge level: 1–5: Ideas and insights:

---

## Wednesday, October 7th

**Mission completed?** Challenge level: 1–5: Ideas and insights:

## Thursday, October 8th

The Moon moves into Cancer.
Power surge for those with stamps in Aries and Cancer.

**Mission completed?** Challenge level: 1–5: Ideas and insights:

## Friday, October 9th

**Mission completed?** Challenge level: 1–5: Ideas and insights:

## Saturday, October 10th

Power surge for those with stamps in Capricorn and Leo.

**Mission completed?** Challenge level: 1–5: Ideas and insights:

## Sunday, October 11th

The Moon moves into Leo.

**Mission completed?** Challenge level: 1–5: Ideas and insights:

# Reflections ...

How did the week's aspiration unfold?

Did you manage to complete your daily meditation?

How easy was it to clear your phone and email?

If you deleted negative communications or people, how did you feel? Did they try to reconnect? This sometimes happens!

List a few things, or even just one, that you are grateful for.

Are there any takeaways from this week that you would like to address next week? Try reflecting without judgment.

# Monday, October 12th–
# Sunday, October 18th

## Forecast

Mercury pumps out a different vibe when it goes retrograde in Scorpio on Wednesday. Don't leave anything undone this week. Delve deeply into projects and anything personal that has been bothering you, for this week will surely trigger you if you swerve to avoid or hide anything. I know it sounds simple, but clearing your space is key to helping you feel more in control, and spending time with people you trust and care for will soothe you. Try not to be too keen to jump into unions with others until you have done enough due diligence on them and found out more about who they are, as opposed to how they make you "feel" about yourself.

This week is a deep one, though, and has fabulous potential for transformation. Venus connects with the Moon midweek, helping us to attract "clean" people – not just people who wash (although that's important too!), but also people with pure hearts and clean motivations, or at least those who try!

The Sun in Libra overpowers the other planets again when it connects with the Moon in Libra, on Thursday, bringing peace, love and harmony to the fore. The New Moon in Libra is on Friday.

## Mission

- Meditate every morning and imagine white light surrounding you.
- Contemplate what areas of life could do with a good cleanse.
- Buy a water bottle and have water on hand at all times: drink plenty.

- Don't suppress anything, but avoid oversharing.
- Write down your deepest, innermost thoughts and fears and burn the ones that you wish to release.

*Aspiration/mantra:* **Pure heart.**

## Monday, October 12th

Power surge for those with stamps in Virgo and Aries.

**Mission completed?** Challenge level: 1–5: Ideas and insights:

## Tuesday, October 13th

The Moon moves into Virgo.

**Mission completed?** Challenge level: 1–5: Ideas and insights:

## Wednesday, October 14th

Mercury goes retrograde in Scorpio. This aspect can be fabulous if we allow past hurts to leave our psyches and forgive ourselves, and others, for mistakes and wrongs. Delve into the depths and read or speak with friends who have knowledge of spiritual matters.

Power surge for those with stamps in Capricorn, Scorpio and Libra.

**Mission completed?** Challenge level: 1–5: Ideas and insights:

_____

_____

## Thursday, October 15th

The Moon moves into Libra.

**Mission completed?** Challenge level: 1–5: Ideas and insights:

_____

_____

## Friday, October 16th

On this day, in 1854, the poet and playwright Oscar Wilde was born.

### New Moon in Libra (3:32 PM EDT)

Ritual time! You may now plant potent seeds for love relationships and business partnerships.

- Focus on what you want and what you are grateful for.
- Write it all down as a list. Contemplate it all as an actual reality.
- Burn the list. Thank the Moon!

Power surge for those with stamps in Capricorn and Scorpio.

**Mission completed?** Challenge level: 1–5: Ideas and insights:

---

## Saturday, October 17th

The Moon moves into Scorpio.

**Mission completed?** Challenge level: 1–5: Ideas and insights:

---

## Sunday, October 18th

Power surge for those with stamps in Capricorn and Sagittarius.

**Mission completed?** Challenge level: 1–5: Ideas and insights:

---

# Reflections ...

How did the week's aspiration unfold?

Did you manage to complete your daily meditation?

How was the New Moon ritual?

List a few things, or even just one, that you are grateful for.

Are there any takeaways from this week that you would like to address next week? Try reflecting without judgment.

# Monday, October 19th– Sunday, October 25th

## Forecast

There is no escape from the intensity of the planets' movements this week, which is absolutely fine for those who enjoy enormous depth, as in penetrating conversations and intense experiences, connections and interactions. Everything lightens up next week, so hold steady and use this week to get your s**t together, but don't get sucked into a bottomless abyss of ambition. Life is short and precious, and while ambition is great, you must beware of becoming short-sighted.

There could be an internal, fierce drive to achieve and succeed right now, so try not to push yourself too hard: be in the moment and keep your serotonin levels high. Laugh, and find joy in knowledge and interactions that will nourish you.

## Mission

Meditate every single day for at least ten minutes. Ask your partner to join you, if you have one, or, if you don't, join a local meditation group. Make a point of meditating with others, as this will magnify the energy.

*Aspiration/mantra:* **I am already successful.**

## Monday, October 19th

The Moon moves into Sagittarius.

**Mission completed?** Challenge level: 1–5: Ideas and insights:

---

---

## Tuesday, October 20th

**Mission completed?** Challenge level: 1–5: Ideas and insights:

---

---

## Wednesday, October 21st

The Moon moves into Capricorn.
Power surge for those with stamps in Capricorn and Libra.

**Mission completed?** Challenge level: 1–5: Ideas and insights:

---

---

## Thursday, October 22nd

The Sun moves into Scorpio.
Saturn, Pluto and Jupiter connect with the Moon. Today is going to hold colossal power and also the potential for transformation, particularly in the areas of work, business, career and serious relationships. Intense energy for all!

**Mission completed?** Challenge level: 1–5: Ideas and insights:

---

## Friday, October 23rd

Power surge for those with stamps in Capricorn and Aquarius.

**Mission completed?** Challenge level: 1–5: Ideas and insights:

---

## Saturday, October 24th

Power surge for those with stamps in Pisces and Aries.

**Mission completed?** Challenge level: 1–5: Ideas and insights:

---

## Sunday, October 25th

The Moon moves into Pisces.

**Mission completed?** Challenge level: 1–5: Ideas and insights:

---

# Reflections ...

How did the week's aspiration unfold?

_____

_____

Did you manage to complete your daily meditation?

_____

_____

Did you notice any difference when the Sun moved from Libra to join Mercury in Scorpio?

_____

_____

List a few things, or even just one, that you are grateful for.

_____

_____

Are there any takeaways from this week that you would like to address next week? Try reflecting without judgment.

_____

_____

# Monday, October 26th–Saturday, October 31st

## Forecast

Plenty of shifts this week leading us back toward Libra, which is really good, as it lightens the vibe and enables us to enjoy socializing.

Venus moves into Libra, and Mercury is still retrograde, but changes sign from Scorpio into Libra.

We celebrate Halloween this week (also known as All Hallows' Eve) and we have a Blue Moon on the same day, so its power is seriously profound! Halloween used to be on the same day as the Christian festival All Saints' Day, but the Vatican blasted the tradition and shifted All Saints' Day to November 1st instead. Halloween was derived from an ancient festival called Samhain, believed to signal the end of light's half year and the beginning of the dark's half. It was a time when the last crops were harvested and stored and animals were slaughtered. The Celts have long believed that at this halfway mark, the veil between our world and others becomes thinner, thus allowing spirts and demons to pass through. The idea behind dressing up was to fool real ghosts and demons into not recognizing us as mortals.

## Mission

- Meditate every day, for at least ten minutes.

- Exercise every day, in order to increase your serotonin levels. Try to get outside as much as you can, without being plugged into anything electronic. *Breathe!*

- Vanquish your demons by facing your fears and releasing one each day. Send them to the light.

- At midnight on October 31st, light candles and then look in a mirror and try to connect with your own spirit for long enough to extract truth. You may do this as a group or alone.

*Aspiration/mantra:* **I am a pure spirit in a physical body. My eyes are the windows to my soul.**

## Monday, October 26th

**Mission completed?** Challenge level: 1–5: Ideas and insights:

_____

_____

## Tuesday, October 27th

**Mission completed?** Challenge level: 1–5: Ideas and insights:

_____

_____

## Wednesday, October 28th

The Moon moves into Aries.
Mercury goes retrograde in Libra.
Venus moves into Libra.
Power surge for those with stamps in Capricorn and Aries.

**Mission completed?** Challenge level: 1–5: Ideas and insights:

_____

_____

# Thursday, October 29th

**Mission completed?** Challenge level: 1–5: Ideas and insights:

_____

_____

# Friday, October 30th

The Moon moves into Taurus.
Power surge for those with stamps in Libra and Taurus.

**Mission completed?** Challenge level: 1–5: Ideas and insights:

_____

_____

# Saturday, October 31st

**All Hallows' Eve.**

### Full Moon in Taurus (10:49 AM EDT)

- Focus on releasing any low-vibe traits that you wish to vanquish! Greed, jealousy, envy and anger: go for it, write them all down and then burn the list.

**Mission completed?** Challenge level: 1–5: Ideas and insights:

_____

_____

# Reflections ...

How did the week's aspiration unfold?

Did you manage to complete your daily meditation?

Did you vanquish your inner demons?

Did you notice anything different on October 31st?

How was the Blue Moon on All Hallows' Eve?

List a few things, or even just one, that you are grateful for.

Are there any takeaways from this week that you would like to address next week? Try reflecting without judgment.

_____

_____

Take a few moments to acknowledge your spiritual self and just be before you move on to November.

_____

_____

# November

"November" comes from the Latin word *novem*, meaning "nine," because in the ancient Roman calendar, before January and February were added, November was the ninth and penultimate month. Now, obviously it's the eleventh month and, in numerology, this is a master number and one that increases the potential for spiritual evolution. When eleven is joined to create a single-digit number (1 + 1), it forms the number two. In numerology, two is the number that indicates an extremely emotional and intuitive person or time. It is linked to the Enchanter, or the Enchantress, the one who sees through the veil and is able to use their knowledge to control a subject or situation, which is very aligned with Scorpio's superpowers.

November is also code for the letter "N" in radio and covert communications, which are typical of this time of year (a.k.a. Scorpio season): codes, betrayals, secrets and spells all abound in the sign, and at the time, that the occult uses most.

This is because Scorpio is a seriously potent sign and time, holding the most potential for transformation on so many levels. There is a lot of energy directing us toward passion, and this can either be directed into basic, materialistic and animalistic pleasures, or used to raise the bar and attract deep, soul-penetrating unions and transformative situations.

It's possible to bump into soul mates and soul enemies at this time, so be discerning before you open up to those that you may not yet know in this life: find out who they might be behind the mask.

## Signs in the Spotlight

 *Scorpio* (also its opposite sign, *Taurus*, to a lesser degree).

 *Libra* (also its opposite sign, *Aries*, to a lesser degree).

 *Sagittarius* (also its opposite sign, *Gemini*, to a lesser degree).

 *Capricorn* (also its opposite sign, *Cancer*, to a lesser degree).

# Pluto in Capricorn: Spiritual Revolution

Pluto influences Scorpio greatly. Some astrologers say that it's the sign's ruler, while others insist that this is Mars. I believe Scorpio people align more with either one or the other. Pluto is now direct in the sign of Capricorn. Under this alignment we are asked to delve deep, master our intuition and gut instincts and begin our training if we wish to be a part of the spiritual revolution. Many people have the ability to intuit things or even at times to seem prophetic, and this comes with the greatest responsibility, for, unless the motivation is correct and wisdom cultivated, the karma generated can be catastrophic. Misusing influence or power is the surest route to endless suffering.

Those who succumb solely to their baser instincts will also fall victim to narcissistic habits. However, folks like you, who consciously choose to jump off the carousel, can decide to contribute toward saving the planet instead, and in doing so raise the vibrations with the rest of the warriors. We all have the choice, and we should leave others to make their own choice rather than set ourselves up as judge and jury. That way we will conserve our energy for the coming shift; indeed, we will need it if we are to stay positive and active and, above all else, operate with loving kindness. That is the path.

November 2020 is a deep one, without doubt. Pluto in Capricorn asks that we transform our own thinking and ambitions and look at the much bigger, and deeper, picture. This can only be achieved by working on ourselves from the inside out.

The beginning of the month is owned by Scorpio, as the Sun is in that sign until the 21st, charging us all up with its insightful clarity and power (especially those with major stamps in Scorpio). How we use this power is up to us. Which wolf do we choose to feed? The responsibility lies with us. The blame game, remember, is one for losers. For certainly nobody will be hailed as the winner.

We do not know what profound lessons lie within the darker side of Scorpio and its opposite sign, Taurus; we do not know what karma we need to purify or what opportunities may be buried in adversity, but this month is brimming with the potential to bust through some past-life issues and allow our crystalline light to be revealed. This is the power that Pluto holds.

# Hypnotic Appeal

Scorpio is both the most feared and the most revered sign and time of the zodiac for good reason. Power, sex appeal and magnetism are there for the taking right now. As are certain powers that, when used correctly, can hypnotize anyone and manipulate any situation. Of course, great power always walks in tandem with the darker sides of life, such as jealousy, greed, anger and envy. These are demons that exist inside us all to a greater or lesser extent, and we can either allow people to arouse them in us, or we can vanquish them with self-study and the drive to do good! We have to use our own power as a force for good and avoid engaging in any battles for supremacy. These battles are rife during Scorpio season.

# The Planets

As we begin the month, the Sun is in Scorpio, while Jupiter, Saturn and Pluto are direct in Capricorn, Uranus is retrograde in Taurus (for the whole month), Neptune is retrograde in Pisces until the 29th and Venus is in Libra, which chills out the intensity somewhat. Venus then moves to join Scorpio on the 21st, impacting the individual and collective heart. This brings the capacity to empathize, though, which is fabulous.

# Practice, Practice, Practice

Now, more than ever, we need a medication practice to keep our mind steady. The energies of the planets are intensifying as we prepare for the serious reboot of the Age of Aquarius next month. We must train mentally, spiritually and also physically if we are to play our part, and we must keep the vibes high and positive. Spiritual practice will ensure that we are able to navigate the swirling energies, riding those waves and dancing to the rhythms of life with both skill and determination. There is little point working out to give yourself the perfect body if your mind is not peaceful and strong, and so this month, and going forward, we must all delve deeply into our spiritual practices and set a precedent for the coming shift in consciousness. It's vital not to get too caught up in worldly affairs and skip mind-training and prayer. If we do, we are likely to miss the major opportunities for growth that are masquerading as challenges or miss the universe's subtle requests to transform.

*Scorpio's mantra:* **I embrace my power and use it as a force for good.**

# Sunday, November 1st– Sunday, November 8th

## Forecast

Mercury shifts its energetic output and goes direct in the beautiful sign of Libra until November 10th, when it moves to align with Scorpio. In Libra, it connects with Venus and this lightens the intensity of Scorpio's rule. This combination also highlights the need for us to find calm and peace on a deeper level.

It's likely to be a busy week and there will be fabulous opportunities for socializing and making connections, but knowing when to retreat is vital for the conservation of our chi (life force). By becoming more diplomatic and skillfully navigating our way through situations, we will boost our inner calm, which will help us to find balance. Heal any rifts in situations or relationships at this time. The Sun in Scorpio is asking us to become more empathetic and bring our true nature into the light.

## Mission

- Meditate every day for fifteen minutes. Set an alarm and use your breath as your focus.
- Don't speak negatively to anyone, including yourself; if you do, make a move to bring peace to the situation immediately.

*Aspiration/mantra:* **I have a peaceful heart and mind.**

## Sunday, November 1st

The Moon is in Taurus.

**Mission completed?** Challenge level: 1–5: Ideas and insights:

_____

_____

## Monday, November 2nd

The Moon moves into Gemini.
Power surge for those with stamps in Capricorn and Gemini.

**Mission completed?** Challenge level: 1–5: Ideas and insights:

_____

_____

## Tuesday, November 3rd

Mercury goes direct in Libra.

**Mission completed?** Challenge level: 1–5: Ideas and insights:

_____

_____

# Wednesday, November 4th

The Moon moves into Cancer.
Power surge for those with stamps in Libra and Cancer.

**Mission completed?** Challenge level: 1–5: Ideas and insights:

---

# Thursday, November 5th

Known as Bonfire Night or Guy Fawkes Night in the UK, and also called National Disobedience Day by some, it's a celebration commemorating the failed Gunpowder Plot. Catholic Guy Fawkes was caught before he had carried out the plan to blow up London's Houses of Parliament and murder the new Protestant king, James I, in 1605. The plot was uncovered when an anonymous letter was sent to the authorities and, when the Houses of Parliament were searched, enough gunpowder was found to blow up half of Westminster. Today, use the tradition to purify your life and carry out a purging ritual of your own: make a list of all the things that you wish to purify and burn it (safely).

**Mission completed?** Challenge level: 1–5: Ideas and insights:

---

# Friday, November 6th

**Mission completed?** Challenge level: 1–5: Ideas and insights:

## Saturday, November 7th

The Moon moves into Leo.
Power surge for those with stamps in Libra and Leo.

**Mission completed?** Challenge level: 1–5: Ideas and insights:

---

---

## Sunday, November 8th

**Mission completed?** Challenge level: 1–5: Ideas and insights:

---

---

# Reflections ...

How did the week's aspiration unfold?

---

---

Did you manage to complete your daily meditation?

---

---

Did you manage to give pleasure without expectation?

---

---

List a few things, or even just one, that you are grateful for.

Are there any takeaways from this week that you would like to address next week? Try reflecting without judgment.

# Monday, November 9th– Sunday, November 15th

## Forecast

Venus remains in Libra and Mercury shifts into Scorpio on Tuesday. Our communications intensify when this happens, becoming deeper and more probing, profound even. It's delicious, unless you're channeling the low vibe of Scorpio stuck in the past, playing the blame game. Be mindful in both your thoughts and your communications.

The Moon moves into Libra and connects with Venus, giving opportunities to enjoy pleasure in its entirety, but balance is also important. If you are already in an intimate union, make an effort to serve your partner's needs and ask them to do the same for you. Don't give just to receive, though – see how much pleasure you can bring to your loved ones and, indeed, anyone in your life. Grand gestures are unnecessary; kindness and the ability to listen to others and intuit their needs are more rewarding than anything else.

Mercury in Scorpio connects with the Moon at the tail end of the week and this is ideal for investing in projects and people that evoke passion.

## Mission

- Meditate daily for fifteen minutes. Don't allow excuses to prevent you from spending time with your mind.

- Develop the habit of checking your motivation before you do, or say, anything. Check your intentions even before you send an email or text message, and be honest about why you are doing, or saying, something. If you can learn to adopt this habit, it can be life changing!

*Aspiration/mantra:* **Check your motivation.**

## Monday, November 9th

The Moon moves into Virgo.
Power surge for those with stamps in Libra and Virgo.

**Mission completed?** Challenge level: 1–5: Ideas and insights:

## Tuesday, November 10th

Mercury moves into Scorpio. Communication becomes intense. Be careful not to obsess, and learn how to let go.

**Mission completed?** Challenge level: 1–5: Ideas and insights:

## Wednesday, November 11th

The Moon moves into Libra.
Power surge for those with stamps in Capricorn and Libra.

**Mission completed?** Challenge level: 1–5: Ideas and insights:

## Thursday, November 12th

Jupiter forms an exact conjunction with Pluto in Capricorn. This is a wonderful time to focus on marriage, as well as career and commitments in general. It also brings the opportunity to master our emotions, keep those that are helpful and leave behind the rest.

**Mission completed?** Challenge level: 1–5: Ideas and insights:

---

---

## Friday, November 13th

The Moon moves into Scorpio.
Power surge for those with stamps in Capricorn and Scorpio.

**Mission completed?** Challenge level: 1–5: Ideas and insights:

---

---

## Saturday, November 14th

Mars goes direct in Aries. This brings a major energy boost, especially for those with stamps in Aries. Be careful not to argue with people or become competitive, though, as Mars opposes Venus over the next few days. Exercise instead and temper the temper!
Power surge for those with stamps in Aries.

**Mission completed?** Challenge level: 1–5: Ideas and insights:

---

---

## Sunday, November 15th

---

### New Moon in Scorpio (12:07 AM EST)

Ritual time! This one is about our deeper intentions.

- Make a list of your dreams and aspirations and focus on spiritual practice, as its power is magnified today and your potential for transformation is immense.

- Burn the list and release your wishes, with faith that the universe will assist those with sincere intentions.

---

The Moon moves into Sagittarius.
Power surge for those with stamps in Scorpio, Capricorn and Sagittarius.

**Mission completed?** Challenge level: 1–5: Ideas and insights:

_____

_____

# Reflections ...

How did the week's aspiration unfold?

_____

_____

Did you manage to complete your daily meditation?

_____

_____

Did you manage to check your motivation before sending emails and other forms of communication?

Did you notice anything different when Mercury moved to join the Sun in Scorpio?

How was the energy of the New Moon in Scorpio?

List a few things, or even just one, that you are grateful for.

Are there any takeaways from this week that you would like to address next week? Try reflecting without judgment.

# Monday, November 16th–
# Sunday, November 22nd

## Forecast

Venus moves into Scorpio, which is incredible if you are ready to deepen your love, and connections in general. It can also trigger old flames, and revelations and relationship issues from the past. Avoid being sucked into illusory thinking or power plays, driven by jealousy. Venus is all about love, and when it joins Scorpio, it can translate as a love of control, so be careful not to operate with this driving your subconscious but have compassion for those who do and do not lower your guard.

## Mission

In order to progress with our life, we often have to heal the past. This week is prime time to do just that. Revisit any issues with partners and money and focus on changing old habits and healing wounds.

- Meditate every day for at least fifteen minutes.

- Write a list of any disruptive patterns that you notice relating to love and money. Do it on paper that you can burn at the end of the week.

- Exercise every day, even if it's only walking for ten minutes.

- Unplug from your phone and emails each night at the same time and just be with yourself, or your loved ones, without external distractions.

*Aspiration/mantra:* **I attract deep soul love.**

## Monday, November 16th

**Mission completed?** Challenge level: 1–5: Ideas and insights:

## Tuesday, November 17th

The Moon moves into Capricorn.
Power surge for those with stamps in Sagittarius and Capricorn.

**Mission completed?** Challenge level: 1–5: Ideas and insights:

## Wednesday, November 18th

**Mission completed?** Challenge level: 1–5: Ideas and insights:

## Thursday, November 19th

The Moon moves into Aquarius.
Power surge for those with stamps in Sagittarius and Aquarius.

**Mission completed?** Challenge level: 1–5: Ideas and insights:

## Friday, November 20th

**Mission completed?** Challenge level: 1–5: Ideas and insights:

---

---

## Saturday, November 21st

The Sun moves into Sagittarius.
Venus moves into Scorpio.
Power surge for those with stamps in Aries and Pisces.

**Mission completed?** Challenge level: 1–5: Ideas and insights:

---

---

## Sunday, November 22nd

The Moon moves into Pisces.

**Mission completed?** Challenge level: 1–5: Ideas and insights:

---

---

# Reflections ...

How did the week's aspiration unfold?

---

---

Did you manage to complete your daily meditation?

_____

_____

Did you notice any disruptive patterns from the past? Burn the list and allow the inspiration to flood in after the release.

_____

_____

Did you feel a lightness when the Sun changed signs into Sagittarius?

_____

_____

List a few things, or even just one, that you are grateful for.

_____

_____

Are there any takeaways from this week that you would like to address next week? Try reflecting without judgment.

_____

_____

# Monday, November 23rd–
# Monday, November 30th

## Forecast

The energy of Neptune and the Full Moon takes precedence this week and is likely to be in full flow by the weekend. When Neptune goes direct, after a long retrograde journey in Pisces, we have the chance to align with a higher vision again and to really concentrate our efforts on our spiritual path. The Full Moon is in Gemini, so list one negative thought that comes into your mind each day and also any fears.

## Mission

Use the energy of the Full Moon on Monday the 30th, to conduct a major release of any habits relating to communications that can hold you back.

*Aspiration/mantra:* **I am a positive person.**

## Monday, November 23rd

**Mission completed?** Challenge level: 1–5: Ideas and insights:

_____

_____

# Tuesday, November 24th

The Moon moves into Aries.
Power surge for those with stamps in Aries and Capricorn.

**Mission completed?** Challenge level: 1–5: Ideas and insights:

_____

_____

# Wednesday, November 25th

**Mission completed?** Challenge level: 1–5: Ideas and insights:

_____

_____

# Thursday, November 26th

Power surge for those with stamps in Capricorn and Taurus.

**Mission completed?** Challenge level: 1–5: Ideas and insights:

_____

_____

# Friday, November 27th

The Moon moves into Taurus.

**Mission completed?** Challenge level: 1–5: Ideas and insights:

_____

_____

# Saturday, November 28th

**Mission completed?** Challenge level: 1–5: Ideas and insights:

_____

_____

# Sunday, November 29th

The Moon moves into Gemini.
Neptune goes direct in Pisces.
Power surge for those with stamps in Capricorn and Gemini.

**Mission completed?** Challenge level: 1–5: Ideas and insights:

_____

_____

# Monday, November 30th

## Full Moon in Gemini (4:29 AM EST)

Ritual time!

- Make a list of all the negative thoughts and forms of communication that hold you back.
- Burn them all (safely), visualizing the universe expelling them from your mind and life.
- Refuse to engage with anything, or anyone, toxic, or negative.
- Make a note of any ideas and insights that come to you.

**Mission completed?** Challenge level: 1–5: Ideas and insights:

_____

_____

# Reflections ...

How did the week's aspiration unfold?

_____

_____

Did you manage to complete your daily meditation?

_____

_____

Did you exercise daily?

_____

_____

How was the Full Moon ritual?

_____

_____

List a few things, or even just one, that you are grateful for.

_____

_____

Are there any takeaways from this week that you would like to address next week? Try reflecting without judgment.

Take a few moments to chill with the energy of Neptune and tune in to your imagination before stepping into December. Jot down any ideas you'd like to pursue for the month ahead.

# December

☀

Welcome to December, also known as Sagittarius season. December used to be the tenth month of the year in the Roman calendar, hence being named after the Latin word *decem*, which means "ten." This is the month this whole journal has been gearing up for, in order to prepare you for the Age of Aquarius. I believe that this new age takes an enormous stride forward on December 19th, when Jupiter moves into the sign of Aquarius and joins Saturn there for the first time since 1964. A few areas of your life may need to be adjusted, and it may even be uncomfortable, but if you dream of a more united world, one where we help one another and desire to form a more compassionate society, know that the time is now.

Sagittarius, as a sign and time, is the one with the most potential for learning and adventure (indeed, some say the two are intrinsically linked) and the one that loves to seek new pastures to feed the mind with deeper truths and spiritual knowledge. It's the sign of the teacher, the mentor and the prophet, but wisdom and humility are required to make the most of its influence.

## Signs in the Spotlight

 *Sagittarius* (also its opposite sign, *Gemini*, to a lesser degree).

 *Capricorn* (also its opposite sign, *Cancer*, to a lesser degree, until the Full Moon in Cancer on December 30th).

 *Scorpio* (also its opposite sign *Taurus*, to a lesser degree).

*Aries* (also its opposite sign, *Libra*, to a lesser degree).

# Luck and Longevity

Sagittarius is the ninth sign of the zodiac, and in Chinese the number nine means "lucky" and represents longevity; certainly anything we learn at this time will stand us in good stead for enjoying good fortune. There is definitely the potential to be lucky this season, especially if you have plenty of Sagittarius in your chart, but there is also the danger of overindulgence. This is not the way of the spiritual warrior and only leads to houses made of cards that are sure to come crashing down.

Because we are in the tenth month of the Roman calendar, though, the numerology of December indicates divinity and the potential to achieve greatness. If we balance our self-interest with the needs of the wider community, we will be walking our true soul's path.

# Seek Inspiration

Study this month: seek out teachings and inspire your mind with sacred wisdom. Find a real teacher who has studied with masters and then has taken the very first step toward enlightenment. This is the only way to liberate our minds and align with the collective soul. We then realize that this is only one life of many and the more we can do to expand our consciousness, the better in the long run ... and it is, indeed, a very, very long run. There is no quick fix; don't believe anyone who says that they have the power to purify your karma, only you have the ability to do that. You do it by becoming more aware and seizing opportunities to become a better, stronger, more rounded human being with a clean heart and soul. You don't have to follow a religion. Some religions focus more on "them and us" divides and they often direct us to seek externally and find the answers in faraway places rather than within. We all have higher consciousness residing in our hearts, minds and souls, and all we need do is to trigger its awakening and face ourselves honestly. Sagittarius, as a sign and time, loves the concept of truth and this is the month to study and bring the more profound truths back to our own mind.

# The Archer of Truth

We still have a very strong Scorpio influence this month, due to Venus being in Scorpio until the 15th, when it moves into Sagittarius and the Archer of Truth is poised to hit our heart. When this alignment goes wrong, we blame others for where we are in our life and fail to understand why or how something played out as it did. If someone hurts us or even betrays us, we must thank them for taking the time to teach us. That doesn't mean that we have to continue our association or allow the hurt to remain; it does mean that we have the opportunity to extract the lesson, delve into the mysterious realms where pure truth lies and purify our own karma, depending on how we handle it. Forgiving and moving on is the best way. If we lower our vibe to envy, jealousy or even bitterness, we lose step with the revolution and stand to miss out on so much. Don't get left behind.

# The Way of the Warrior

If you meditate daily and have a strong spiritual practice, you begin to realize that each and every challenging person or situation that you face is 50 percent down to you, your past karma and your present-day reactions, and only 50 percent down to them. However, true spiritual practitioners realize that it is actually 100 percent down to us. This is the way of the warrior and the path to enlightenment and, trust me, it's what we all aspire to, whether consciously or not. It can only happen if we work for it – this one is never ever handed to us on a plate – but when we begin to catch glimpses of it, as we will, we will be spurred on to work even harder. Trust me, it's incredible.

# Truth and Integrity

Listening to our own truth is vital for well-being and happiness, and with both the Sun and Mercury in Sagittarius and a solar eclipse and the New Moon happening on December 14th, the Sagittarian vibe is pushing for each of us to seek and reveal our true self. Then our vibe will attract our soul tribe and allow us to make real moves that matter. Life is too short not to listen to our heart, and doing the right thing at all times is the only way to purify and sleep well at night. We all have a responsibility to one other and our Divine Mother, and the future is now in our hands. We need to unite. Let's do it now.

# The Planets

Mercury and the Sun are in Sagittarius until the 21st, when the Sun moves into Capricorn, joining Jupiter, Pluto and Saturn until the 17th, when Saturn moves into Aquarius, and the 19th, when Jupiter moves into Aquarius, too, for the first time since the 1960s. This is the shift! Meditation is your seatbelt and compassion the way forward. We must act now to help our Divine Mother and our brothers and sisters. If you wish to adopt changes in your habits, then re-read May (Taurus season). This will help elevate your soul and, trust me, it's an incomparable elevation. Stay steady! Be positive, be kind and let's make sure no one gets left behind.

*Aspiration/mantra:* **I speak my truth, with purpose. Viva revolution!**

# Tuesday, December 1st– Sunday, December 6th

## Forecast

This week should be splendid, brimming with optimism and excitement. The Sun in Sagittarius connects with Mercury in Sagittarius and this will result in a brightness that we all sorely need. Mercury governs the collective mind and so, whatever is going on there, it has a ripple effect across the planet and we will all have the opportunity to catch some feels. The planet moves from Scorpio into Sagittarius this week and this lightens the mood and brings hopefulness.

## Mission

- Meditate for fifteen minutes each morning before you look at your phone.
- Seek optimism each day. When faced with challenges or negative people; flip your own and their minds to positive.

*Aspiration/mantra:* **Optimism!**

## Tuesday, December 1st

On this day in 1955, one black woman refused to accept racial segregation any longer. Rosa Parks was arrested, in Alabama, for refusing to give up her seat to a white man and move to the back of the bus. This was an early protest in the modern American civil rights movement.
The Moon is in Gemini.

Mercury moves into Sagittarius.
Neptune empowers Cancer. If you have stamps in the sign, use the energy to leave disappointments behind and conjure up a fresh vision.
Power surge for those with stamps in Cancer, Gemini, Sagittarius and Pisces.

**Mission completed?** Challenge level: 1–5: Ideas and insights:

# Wednesday, December 2nd

The Moon moves into Cancer.

**Mission completed?** Challenge level: 1–5: Ideas and insights:

# Thursday, December 3rd

**Mission completed?** Challenge level: 1–5: Ideas and insights:

# Friday, December 4th

The Moon moves into Leo.
Power surge for those with stamps in Capricorn and Leo.

**Mission completed?** Challenge level: 1–5: Ideas and insights:

## Saturday, December 5th

Power surge for those with stamps in Aries and Virgo.

**Mission completed?** Challenge level: 1–5: Ideas and insights:

---

---

## Sunday, December 6th

The Moon moves into Virgo.

**Mission completed?** Challenge level: 1–5: Ideas and insights:

---

---

# Reflections ...

How did the week's aspiration unfold?

---

---

Did you feel Mercury's shift into Sagittarius?

---

---

Can you think of one situation when you consciously flipped your own, or someone else's, mind from negative to optimistic?

_____

_____

List a few things, or even just one, that you are grateful for.

_____

_____

Are there any takeaways from this week that you would like to address next week? Try reflecting without judgment.

_____

_____

# Monday, December 7th– Sunday, December 13th

## Forecast

This week offers plenty of potential for socializing and starting celebrations. No matter what your belief system or particular faith, the buzz of the pending season, brimming with holiday fever, will be hard to avoid.

If you live in the northern hemisphere it will be darker for longer with the diminishing hours of daylight, so do all that you can to boost your serotonin levels. Exercise, go for walks, and indulge your creative side: make playlists, draw, paint, write or take photos of things that inspire you. Because there is still a strong Capricorn influence, you may be more somber than usual and prone to be hard on yourself; avoid that and be creative without expectations of world recognition.

## Mission

- Meditate every day for at least fifteen minutes.
- Practice basic Yoga moves every morning at home:
  - Stand with your feet firmly on the ground, arms by your sides, palms facing upward.
  - Inhale. Sweep your arms up and join your hands in prayer position (Anjali Mudra) above your head. Look up at your thumbs.
  - Stretch up! Exhale. Bring your hands in front of your chest in prayer.
  - Repeat several times.
- Find a poem you love (I chose "The Desiderata") and print it out. Frame it and place it by your front door so that you read it before you leave the house.

*Aspiration/mantra:* **Be creative.**

# Monday, December 7th

**Mission completed?** Challenge level: 1–5: Ideas and insights:

---

# Tuesday, December 8th

Power surge for those with stamps in Capricorn and Libra.

**Mission completed?** Challenge level: 1–5: Ideas and insights:

---

# Wednesday, December 9th

The Moon moves into Libra.

**Mission completed?** Challenge level: 1–5: Ideas and insights:

---

# Thursday, December 10th

**Hanukkah starts.**
Literally translated, Hanukkah means "Dedication." This eight-day Jewish festival commemorates the rededication of the Second Temple after the few had defeated the many while fighting for their religious freedoms. The lighting of candles each night of the festival represents a light that lasts beyond expectations in the

darkest of times. The main practice undertaken now is to dedicate yourself to something or some cause.

**Human Rights Day.**

**Mission completed?** Challenge level: 1-5: Ideas and insights:

_____

_____

# Friday, December 11th

The Moon moves into Scorpio.
Power surge for those with stamps in Capricorn and Scorpio.

**Mission completed?** Challenge level: 1-5: Ideas and insights:

_____

_____

# Saturday, December 12th

**Mission completed?** Challenge level: 1-5: Ideas and insights:

_____

_____

# Sunday, December 13th

The Moon moves into Sagittarius.
Power surge for those with stamps in Capricorn and Sagittarius.

**Mission completed?** Challenge level: 1-5: Ideas and insights:

_____

_____

# Reflections ...

How did the week's aspiration unfold?

_____

_____

Did you practice the simple daily Yoga moves on page 302, or any of your own?

_____

_____

Did you channel your creative side?

_____

_____

List a few things, or even just one, that you are grateful for.

_____

_____

Are there any takeaways from this week that you would like to address next week? Try reflecting without judgment.

_____

_____

# Monday, December 14th– Sunday, December 20th

## Forecast

It's about to get hectic, as Saturn moves into Aquarius on Thursday, and it's there to stay until 2023. Then on Saturday Jupiter moves into Aquarius, too. Aquarius is gearing up for revolution and we need to prepare, but until then it's vital that we stay steady and aware, especially as at the moment Sagittarius is the sign with the most influence, and this can be like an energizer bunny, and Aquarius, as a sign, is a little like New York – it never sleeps. We really must, though, otherwise we run the risk of frying our minds, and burning out. This is going to impact us all, but it's even stronger for those with Sagittarius and Aquarius stamps.

## Mission

- Meditate every day for at least ten to fifteen minutes in the same spot.

- Remove all electrical items from your bedroom: it's essential in order to rest your energy and chemistry. Leave your phone and laptop in another room when you sleep.

- Take at least twenty to thirty minutes each morning before you "plug in." This routine will protect you and your energy.

Note: If you have children, teaching them how to protect and care for their energy is one of the best things that you can do, so try this mission as a family. If you have a partner, don't dictate to them, but tell them that you need this routine and really would appreciate their support (it will help them, too, but let's stick to the not preaching or dictating plan).

*Aspiration/mantra:* **Unplug.**

## Monday, 14th December

### New Moon in Sagittarius (11:17 AM EST)

New Moon ritual!

- Set your positive intentions and write them down.
- Think of someone you know who may be feeling low and add to your list a request that their spirits are lifted and their optimism returned.

**Total Solar Eclipse (8:33 AM EST)**
This is when the New Moon comes between the Earth and the Sun, casting its darkest shadows on the Earth; it's likely the daylight will disappear for a few moments, turning day into night. Don't worry – night is simply the time when the Sun takes a back seat and gives the Moon some time to shine.
Mercury connects with the Moon.
Power surge for those with stamps in Capricorn and Sagittarius.

**Mission completed?** Challenge level: 1–5: Ideas and insights:

## Tuesday, December 15th

The Moon moves into Capricorn.
Venus moves into Sagittarius.

**Mission completed?** Challenge level: 1–5: Ideas and insights:

## Wednesday, December 16th

**Mission completed?** Challenge level: 1–5: Ideas and insights:

---

---

## Thursday, December 17th

The Moon moves into Aquarius.
Saturn moves into Aquarius.
Power surge for those with stamps in Sagittarius, Capricorn and Aquarius.

**Mission completed?** Challenge level: 1–5: Ideas and insights:

---

---

## Friday, December 18th

**Hanukkah ends.**

**Mission completed?** Challenge level: 1–5: Ideas and insights:

---

---

## Saturday, December 19th

The Moon moves into Pisces.
Jupiter moves into Aquarius.
Power surge for those with stamps in Sagittarius and Pisces.

**Mission completed?** Challenge level: 1–5: Ideas and insights:

_____

_____

## Sunday, December 20th

Mercury moves into Capricorn.

**Mission completed?** Challenge level: 1–5: Ideas and insights:

_____

_____

# Reflections ...

How did the week's aspiration unfold?

_____

_____

Did you set positive intentions under the New Moon?

_____

_____

Did you manage to unplug?

_____

_____

Did you feel any different when Saturn switched signs to Aquarius?

_____

_____

How about when Jupiter joined it?

_____

_____

List a few things, or even just one, that you are grateful for.

_____

_____

Are there any takeaways from this week that you would like to address next week? Try reflecting without judgment.

_____

_____

# Monday, December 21st–Sunday, December 27th

## Forecast

The Sun switches signs and joins Mercury in Capricorn. This steadies the Uranian rule somewhat, but the vibe is still eclectic and random. It is the holiday week and whether you celebrate Christmas or not, use this time to celebrate humanity and to reconnect with people you care about. If you are not planning on sitting down and eating way too much food on Friday (that will be hard, as the Moon will be in Taurus, and Taurus loves to chow-down on delicious food and enjoy the finest of tipples) just cook for others, and focus on distributing kindness and nourishment with love.

## Mission

- Meditate every day, for at least ten minutes.
- Volunteer at a food kitchen and give back to those less fortunate. There are charities that will help you to do this, or you can just do it yourself. Sadly, there are always homeless people suffering on the streets.
- Focus on goodwill to all and refuse to engage in any arguments.
- Be patient with your family, come what may.

*Aspiration/mantra:* **I am surrounded with love.**

## Monday, December 21st

The Sun moves into Capricorn.
The Moon moves into Aries.
There is an exact conjunction of Jupiter and Saturn in Aquarius.
Power surge for everyone.

**Mission completed?** Challenge level: 1–5: Ideas and insights:

---

## Tuesday, December 22nd

The Winter Solstice in the northern hemisphere – the shortest day of the year.
The Summer Solstice in the southern hemisphere – the longest day of the year.
Join celebrations today, no matter where you are, or your faith, and take part in positive, light-bringing rituals using prayer and fire.

**Mission completed?** Challenge level: 1–5: Ideas and insights:

---

## Wednesday, December 23rd

Power surge for those with stamps in Aries and Taurus.

**Mission completed?** Challenge level: 1–5: Ideas and insights:

## Thursday, December 24th

**Christmas Eve.**
The Moon moves into Taurus.

**Mission completed?** Challenge level: 1–5: Ideas and insights:

---

## Friday, December 25th

**Christmas Day.**

**Mission completed?** Challenge level: 1–5: Ideas and insights:

---

## Saturday, December 26th

The Moon moves into Gemini.
Power surge for those with stamps in Scorpio, Capricorn and Gemini.

**Mission completed?** Challenge level: 1–5: Ideas and insights:

---

## Sunday, December 27th

**Mission completed?** Challenge level: 1–5: Ideas and insights:

---

# Reflections ...

How did the week's aspiration unfold?

Did you manage to volunteer?

Did you encounter arguments? How did you handle them?

List a few things, or even just one, that you are grateful for.

Are there any takeaways from this week that you would like to address next week? Try reflecting without judgment.

# Monday, December 28th– Thursday, December 31st

## Forecast

We have been blessed with a powerful Full Moon just before we welcome in a new year! On Tuesday we need to release the emotional baggage from the year and surrender to the mystery that awaits! This is a creative process, so add to the list each day: don't rush it. You must forgive the past and relish the present.

## Mission

- Meditate every day, without fail. Choose the morning if you can, before the day takes over.
- Work on having a major Full Moon release by writing a list of all the emotional baggage that you carry around with you. Work on it daily.

*Aspiration/mantra:* **I forgive and move on.**

## Monday, December 28th

**Mission completed?** Challenge level: 1–5: Ideas and insights:

_____

_____

## Tuesday, December 29th

**Full Moon in Cancer (10:28 PM EST).**

Ritual time!

- Cancer is all about emotion; reflect for a moment on how you're feeling today and what you'd like to release to enhance your emotional well-being.
- Take your list and burn it, releasing all the negativity, forgiving all those that you feel have wronged you and purifying everything.

The Moon moves into Cancer.
Power surge for those with stamps in Aries and Cancer.

**Mission completed?** Challenge level: 1–5: Ideas and insights:

## Wednesday, December 30th

Power surge for those with stamps in Aries and Pisces.

**Mission completed?** Challenge level: 1–5: Ideas and insights:

# Thursday, December 31st

**New Year's Eve.**

The Moon moves into Leo. This is a great time for love, laughter and fun! The Moon in Leo expands our hearts and heightens our potential for generosity of spirit. Power surge for those with stamps in Aries and Leo.

**Mission completed?** Challenge level: 1–5: Ideas and insights:

_____

_____

# Reflections ...

How did the week's aspiration unfold?

_____

_____

Did you carry out the Full Moon ritual on Tuesday? How did it make you feel to focus on releasing emotional baggage?

_____

_____

List a few things, or even just one, that you are grateful for.

_____

_____

Are there any takeaways from this week that you would like to address next week? Try reflecting without judgment.

_____

_____

How was 2020 for you?

- Take a few moments to reflect ... and appreciate all the improvements you made and just how much you learned.
- Are you ready for 2021?

# Dedication

When I was a baby, doctors told my parents I may never walk; now I jog daily and run like the wind from drama.

In many of my school reports teachers labeled me as "disruptive." I turned that into a career. I always dreamed of being a writer, but many folks told me I didn't stand a chance ... My second book is dedicated to them.

My point is, believe in yourself, avoid the naysayers, work hard, find your humor and your tribe!

I also wish to sincerely thank everyone who helped me to create this journal, especially my Capricorn mother who still loans me money and treats me like a five-year-old.

I thank each and every person who buys this journal and uses it to elevate their consciousness and share the knowledge, we are all in this life thing together.

Celebrate each and every day you are alive, and reach for the stars; impossible is nothing.

Published under the title
*Your Stars* in the United Kingdom
by HarperCollins in 2019.

Your Signs. © 2019 by Carolyne Faulkner.

Illustrations © Dynamic Astrology Ltd
Endpaper design by HYD Agency
Page design by Hugh Adams

HarperCollins books may be purchased for educational, business,
or sales promotional use. For information please email the
Special Markets Department at SPsales@harpercollins.com.

Published in 2019 by
Harper Design
An *Imprint* of HarperCollins*Publishers*
195 Broadway, New York, NY 10007
Tel: (212) 207-7000
Fax: (855) 746-6023
harperdesign@harpercollins.com
www.hc.com

Distributed throughout the world by
HarperCollins*Publishers*
195 Broadway
New York, New York 10007

ISBN 978-0-06-295564-7

Library of Congress Cataloging-in-Publication Data
has been applied for.

Printed and bound in the USA

First Printing, 2019